SHORT CUTS

INTRODUCTIONS TO FILM STUDIES

OTHER TITLES IN THE SHORT CUTS SERIES

FILM VIOLENCE

HISTORY, IDEOLOGY, GENRE

JAMES KENDRICK

WALLFLOWER

LONDON and NEW YORK

A Wallflower Press Book
Published by
Columbia University Press
Publishers Since 1893
New York   Chichester, West Sussex
cup.columbia.edu

A complete CIP record is available from the Library of Congress

ISBN 978-1-906660-26-0 (pbk. : alk. paper)
ISBN 978-0-231-50220-7 (e-book)

∞

Columbia University Press books are printed on permanent and durable
acid-free paper.

Printed in the United States of America

Cover image: *Taxi Driver* (1976) © Columbia Pictures

CONTENTS

ACKNOWLEDGEMENTS

Slim though it may be, this book is the end result of several years of research, writing, reading, viewing and, importantly, constant dialogue with friends and colleagues, to whom I owe a great deal of thanks for their insight, suggestions and encouragement. Chief among these are my mentors when I was at Indiana University: Joan Hawkins, Barbara Klinger and Chris Anderson, under whose guidance ten years ago I began the initial stages of conceptualising and understanding the multifaceted roles of film violence. I also owe a debt to Eva Cherniavsky and Tom Foster, both of whom read portions of what would eventually become this book. More recently, Joe Kickasola and Bob Rehak were gracious enough to read rough drafts of chapters and provide thoughtful comments, and my good friend Jon Kraszewski offered consistent encouragement and much-needed humour through the long process of researching, writing and publishing.

While working on this book I was blessed to be surrounded by my tremendous colleagues in the Department of Communication Studies at Baylor University, who have been an invaluable source of support and inspiration. In particular, I would like to thank my department chairs Bill English and Dave Schlueter and the Film and Digital Media division heads Michael Korpi and Chris Hansen, all of whom created the kind of stimulating academic environment that makes good work possible. The final stages of writing were also generously supported by a summer sabbatical that was granted by the College of Arts and Sciences and the Provost of Baylor University.

Certainly, this book would have never happened without the generous editors and support staff at Wallflower Press. Yoram Allon was the first to show interest in the project and guide it through its initial stages, and for that I am grateful. My editorial manager Jacqueline Downs was wonderful to work with at every step of the process, and Ian Cooper offered excellent editorial suggestions that helped strengthen key portions of the book.

Most important, love and heartfelt thanks go out to my family, who has always supported my endeavours, and especially to my wonderful wife Cassie, whose constant love, support, inspiration and understanding make everything I do possible.

INTRODUCTION

> The cinema is a peculiarly violent form of entertainment, developed in and catering for what we have come to think of as an age of violence.
>
> Philip French, 'Violence in the Cinema' (1968: 59)

> There is a great streak of violence in every human being. If it is not channelled and understood, it will break out in war and madness.
>
> Sam Peckinpah (quoted in Harmetz 1969: D9)

In an editorial titled 'Growth of the Movies' published on 31 October 1915, the editorial board of the *New York Times* made a bold prediction about the cinema's development that turned out to be utterly and completely wrong. Writing about the 'problem' of the movies, which at that time were in the midst of no small amount of controversy regarding the perceived dangerousness of their moral content, the editorial board noted:

> there is a more reasonable complaint that some of the picture shows deal with violence and crime and have a debasing moral tendency. This last complaint, however, is restricted to a kind which is least likely to endure. We do not believe that the newly created movie public has an inherent liking for this kind … The tendency to depict the ways of criminals and the perpetration of crimes of violence will pass away. It is characteristic of a habit of the hour, and it has been persisted in, probably, because of the pride the movie makers take in their knowledge that they can do such things so well. (Anon. 1915: 16)

As the past 95 years of cinema history have amply shown, violent cinema has not in any sense 'passed away'. In fact, it has not only endured, but flourished, and filmmakers from around the world and across the spectrum of film history have experimented, innovated, played with, subverted and repeated representations of violence onscreen in virtually every genre imaginable. A recent study of box-office performance since the late 1960s has shown a marked increase in the popularity of 'violence-prone genres' both in the US and worldwide (see Lu, Waterman & Yan 2006). As cinematographer John Bailey noted when he caught up on summer movies over the Labor Day weekend in 1994:

> I saw six films along with about two dozen trailers for the autumn releases. Not a single one of the trailers (not to mention the features themselves) was devoid of considerable firepower. I'm not speaking of just action excitement, but of a veritable litany of handgun and automatic weapons discharges, incendiary effects, stabbings, and throat slittings. There were also, of course, a few garrotings and numerous beatings of women. This is studio entertainment, after all. (1994: 26)

As is evident from Bailey's tone, film violence has continued to be a source of social and moral anxiety and controversy, even as it continues to be popular at the box office. A cursory look at the most financially successful US films of the past decade amply illustrates the important role violence, often couched rhetorically as 'action', plays in so many of them: *Titanic* (1997), *Saving Private Ryan* (1998), *Armageddon* (1998), *The Matrix* trilogy (1999–2003), the *Star Wars* prequels (1999–2005), *Gladiator* (2000), *The Lord of the Rings* trilogy (2001–2003), the *Harry Potter* series (2001–2009), the *Spider-Man* series (2002–2007), the *Pirates of the Caribbean* trilogy (2003–2006), *The Passion of the Christ* (2004) and *The Dark Knight* (2008), to name but a few. Of course, each of these films uses violence differently – aesthetically, ideologically and generically – which is precisely why *violence* is such a tricky concept. It is ludicrous to compare the violence of *The Passion of the Christ*, which, however brutally graphic, is borne out of genuine religious and spiritual conviction, with the violence in *Armageddon*, which is designed purely to excite and thrill, yet that is precisely what so many commentators do consciously or unconsciously when they talk about the 'problem' of 'violence in the media'.

The omnipresence of violence in not only the cinema, but in all our mediated forms of entertainment, is one reason why it has remained a crucial topic in media studies and within the general public sphere. However, another reason why we continue to talk about and debate film violence is because talking about violence is a way of talking about other subjects that often get repressed – uncomfortable social and cultural issues such as gender, race, economic disparity, criminality, the perceived dissolution of the public sphere, generational issues, morality, the powerful role of media institutions. In other words, salient cultural issues often get displaced onto discussions and historically determined perceptions of film violence. As J. Hoberman notes, 'spectator antipathy or attraction to screen violence may, in fact, concern something other than the violence itself' (1998: 141). For example, while the graphic levels of violence in Arthur Penn's seminal *Bonnie and Clyde* (1967) would have no doubt raised the ire of many critics and commentators regardless of its narrative, the fact that the film's violence was interwoven into a larger ideological structure that reflected the growing generation gap by encouraging sympathy and identification with the film's young, glamorous, outlaw couple made it all the more potent and therefore dangerous.

The fact that violence, like pornography, is something that is both difficult to define and can bring together the extreme political right and the extreme political left in mutual condemnation is testament to its polysemous nature and cultural salience. The problem is that, when discussing film violence, media scholars and the general public are generally talking about different things, and they are not talking to each other. Media scholars tend to see film violence as a textual strategy that can only be understood by examining it in light of narrative, history and ideology; the aesthetic practices that determine the tone of presentation; and even the ontology of the image itself. The general public, on the other hand, tends to view film violence as a moral and social threat. Their opinions are often shaped by the news media and policymakers who use social science to justify their arguments that media violence constitutes a social ill. Thus, in most public debates, film violence is discussed in terms of the social-scientific pursuit of measuring the effects of viewing mediated violence, an approach that has all but dominated the field and set the terms of the debate. Henry Jenkins, who started the comparative media studies programme at MIT, experienced this firsthand when he accepted an offer to appear on the daily talk show *Donahue* (2002–2003) in 2002 to discuss violence in the media. Although the discussion was specifically about video games, the rhetoric used and the construction of opposing binaries involving the role of violence in entertainment are easily applicable to debates regarding film violence. Jenkins writes, 'This debate always gets presented as though there were only two sides – mothers battling to protect their kids and the cigar-chomping entertainment industry bosses who prey on American youth. This formulation allows no space to defend popular culture from any position other than self-interest' (2002: 2).

Given the salience of this topic in both academic and public circles, it is clear that understanding film violence is central to understanding the social and historical role of the cinema. As J. David Slocum argues, thoughtful enquiry into the nature of film violence 'raises larger questions about whether or how understandings of violence bridge experiences of representations and actual life, about the pleasures of viewing barbarous images or committing actual incidents, and about the necessity to confront destructive tendencies in order to resist or at least comprehend them better' (2001: 3). Thus, in this book I will offer a comprehensive overview of the role violence has played in the cinema from the silent era to the present. I will endeavour to provide a general foundation for understanding film violence from historical, ideological and generic perspectives, which will entail looking at how film violence has affected and been affected by government policies, box-office receipts, gender differences, shifting notions of genre, well-known auteurs, changes in narrative, and broad social trends. My goal is to illustrate in necessarily concise terms the breadth and depth of filmic representations of violence by considering them across both history and geography, although the weight of analysis will focus on films produced in Hollywood, which, since the silent era, has been the most influential and economically successful of national cinemas.

Chapter one will examine the term 'film violence' as a complex signifier that has always been central to film as both art and entertainment. In looking at both the scholarly literature on film violence and the way it has been portrayed in the popular media, I will argue against the idea that film violence is a monolithic 'thing' and will instead present it as a complex mode of signification that needs to be thoroughly grounded in historical, cultural and industrial contexts, as well as subjective experience.

Chapter two will trace filmic depictions of violence from the silent era to the present day, focusing on both aesthetic innovations (special effects, slow-motion and so on) and the various social responses to it. It will reference both films and filmmakers from across the spectrum of film history who were instrumental in defining and redefining the visual, narrative and thematic possibilities of film violence.

Moving from the broad historical outline in the previous chapter, chapter three will focus more closely on how film violence is used in several of the most historically popular film genres (westerns, horror and action). Looking at how representations of violence are used in these specific types of films will show how violence functions ideologically within generic structures and how those ideologies have shifted over time.

Finally, chapter four will offer a specific case study by looking at the centrality of film violence to the young directors of the New American Cinema, with a special emphasis on the 1970s films of Francis Ford Coppola. These filmmakers reworked classical representations of violence to distinguish themselves from the previous generation of Hollywood filmmakers, thus the case study will offer a strong example of how violence, history, ideology and genre are all deeply intertwined.

In sum, this book will offer an examination of film violence from multiple perspectives, including issues of definition, its historical development across world cinema, and how it has been used in and shaped the ideology of popular film genres. The ultimate goal is to demonstrate that film violence is not a simple category or thing. Quite to the contrary, it is a complex set of signifying practices that are indelibly shaped by the subjective experiences of the viewer. Thus, it must be interrogated on multiple fronts – historical, aesthetic, ideological, and so on – which is precisely what I aim to do here. While the book's scope is necessarily limited, my hope is that it will serve as a starting place for those who want to explore and better understand the complexities of film violence, thus continuing the meaningful dialogue begun by others about the role it plays in all of our lives.

1   WHAT DO WE MEAN BY 'FILM VIOLENCE'?

There is in fact no one thing, no chemically isolatable and analysable substance, that is violence, any more than there is one thing
that is sex, even though it is easy to slip into talking as if there
were.

John Fraser, *Violence in the Arts* (1974: 9)

In one of the most oft-quoted passages in film studies, Christian Metz
(1974: 69) asserted that a film is difficult to explain because it is easy to
understand. So it is with film violence.

When talking about this often heated topic, common sense can often
be our greatest enemy. After all, everyone *knows* what violence is. If you
show a reasonable person footage of a fistfight, a shoot-out, a stabbing –
essentially any image in which someone is in some way physically harmed
– he or she will most likely label it *violence*. It is even easier if the violence
is graphic, that is, if it shows blood spattering, flesh ripping and other
visual signs of physical trauma. It is so *obvious*. And yet, the very obvious-
ness of film violence – so visceral, so attention-grabbing, pounding our
senses and cutting right through to our emotional core – often blinds us
to the startling complexities and unexamined assumptions of every cinematic jab, gunshot, fistfight and explosion.

Common sense tells us that we know exactly what violence is, but once
we start unpacking all of the associations, assumptions and elisions of

our own personal definition of the word and comparing it with others, we quickly realise that there is no one *thing* – 'no chemically isolatable and analysable substance', as John Fraser put it – we can call *violence*. Our immediate inclination is to treat violence as a fully- formed and delineated object: something that can be defined, categorised, quantified and, most importantly, *understood* and therefore *controlled*. This has been the aim of the social-scientific discourse that has, until the past 15 years, all but dominated the so-called 'media violence debate'. But it is not that simple. Thinking of film violence as 'given' or 'obvious' or 'common sense' necessarily leads to an ahistorical conception of it and the social roles it has played throughout history.

First, I should be clear that, in discussing film violence throughout this book, I am talking about representations of violence in fictional films, not documented footage of real-life violence that was captured either purposefully or inadvertently on camera. The bloodshed discussed in this book is entirely fabricated through acting, special effects, editing and visual language to suit the needs of a fictional narrative; thus, it does not focus on snuff films, mondo films or atrocity footage, all of which involves documentary presentation of actual events, which is ontologically and epistemologically different from film artists endeavouring to create the illusion of violent actions onscreen for narrative, thematic or aesthetic purposes.[1] Some might argue that the divisions between 'real' and 'reel' violence are not that discreet. Sissela Bok argues that:

> The screen renders experience both less and more real in its own right. It both mediates violence and makes it seem more immediate, exposing viewers to levels and forms of violence they might never otherwise encounter. It helps cross boundaries between real and re-enacted, between art and entertainment, between being near the violence and being at a distance … Questions about degrees of reality and about the role of real-life, imagined, and re-enacted violence in our lives are crucial to our learning to understand and to deal with violence. But these questions cannot be dismissed, much less resolved, by making tidy distinctions between the real and the not-real. (1998: 37)

The implied semantic equivalency in using the term *violence* to describe both actual events and their mediated representations suggests an inherent connection, and some would argue that film violence is a form of actual violence in that it can cause psychological distress and even act directly upon the body, causing revulsion, involuntary muscle spasms and even physical illness.[2] Many of the most infamous violent films are associated with stories, mostly exaggerated, about initial audience members' extreme physical responses. For example, when Sam Peckinpah's *The Wild Bunch* (1969) first screened in a 190-minute rough cut in Kansas City, it was reported that members of the audience left in revulsion and one or two of them vomited in the alleyway behind the theatre (see Harmetz 1969). While I recognise the overlapping of real and re-enacted violence and do not wish to make any overly 'tidy distinctions' between the two, it is also important for our purposes here to draw distinctions in order to maintain some semblance of clarity. Fictional film violence is complicated enough.

Defining film violence

As John Fraser argues in *Violence in the Arts*, the complexity of mediated violence is immense, and it can and has fulfilled numerous and varied functions: 'violence as release, violence as communication, violence as play, violence as self-affirmation, or self-defence, or self-discovery, or self-destruction, violence as a flight from reality, violence as the truest sanity in a particular situation, and so on' (1974: 9). This is essentially Martin Barker's argument when he writes, 'There simply isn't a "thing" called "violence in the media"' (1995: 10). Barker has further noted that the expression 'media violence' is 'one of the most commonly repeated, and one of the most ill-informed, of all time ... *There simply is no category "media violence" which can be researched*' (1997: 27–28; emphasis in original), which is why Barker argues that seventy years of social-scientific effects research has been largely useless: It has been constructed on the faulty logic that there is some such all-encompassing category as 'media violence' that can contain everything from movies, to television shows, to comic books, to newspaper photographs, to video games, to televised news reports and documentary footage.

As it is commonly used, *violence* is an almost uselessly broad term that offers no meaningful distinctions among obviously disparate representations of physical action – a gory disembowelment in a horror film is readily described as 'violent', but so are the cartoon characters Tom and

Jerry hitting each other over the head with frying pans. The simultaneous difference and similarity of such acts is highlighted in parodies such as the 'Itchy & Scratchy' cartoons on *The Simpsons* (1989–present), in which a cat and mouse do terrible physical damage to each other, but with cartoonishly gory, rather than simply cartoonish, results. Having Bart and Lisa Simpson laugh uncontrollably at such images is satirising the sometimes absurd divide we make between suitable violence (not gory) and unsuitable violence (gory), but it is also a pointed example of how even the most gruesome images can be funny when successfully framed as such. Many concerned parties were less appalled by a character's head being shot off in the back seat of a car in *Pulp Fiction* (1994) than they were by Quentin Tarantino's use of such violence as slapstick humour.

When the term *violence* is explicitly defined, it is usually within the confines of social-scientific research, whose methodological approach demands concrete operational definitions. The underlying legitimacy of quantitative enquiry hinges on the researcher's ability to objectively define and therefore quantify that which is being studied. The long-running Cultural Indicators project, one of the foremost studies of media representations of violence and its reception by audiences, has used the broadest of definitions: 'violence was found to be primarily a demonstration of power' (Gerbner, Gross, Morgan & Signorielli 1994: 19). More specifically, project researchers have defined violence as 'the overt expression of physical force against self or other, compelling action against one's will on pain of being hurt or killed, or actually hurting or killing' (Gerbner and Gross 1976: 184). Similarly, David L. Lange, Robert K. Baker and Sandra J. Ball define a violent act as 'The threat or use of force that results, or is intended to result, in the injury or forcible restraint or intimidation of persons, or the destruction or forcible seizure of property' (1969: 235).

Similar definitions have crept into humanistic scholarship on film violence. Even those scholars who seek to complicate the idea of film violence using the kinds of historical, cultural, aesthetic and personal contexts that social-scientific discourse usually eliminates have found it necessary to lay some kind of foundation in defining what, exactly, we are talking about when we talk about film violence. In the introduction to the anthology *Violence and American Cinema*, J. David Slocum warns about the dangers posed by the term *violence*, calling it 'a notoriously expansive notion' (2001: 2). Yet, he still offers a definition of the term that he calls 'the least elaboration' – 'an action or behaviour that is harmful or injurious' (ibid.) – then immediately shows how complex even *that* seemingly simple definition is: the harm can be physical, psychological or sociological; harm need not even be done since the threat of harm can be just as disturbing as the harm itself; the violence can be systematic or structural (for example, racism, sexism and so forth), rather than the product of an individual causal agent; and violence can be seen as an unavoidable aspect of human nature. Most importantly, though, Slocum notes that an action is labelled 'violent' through a web of complex social processes: 'Legitimacy as a critical category is thus crucial not only for the actions it validates as violent within a given culture but for the behaviours that it excludes from popular discourses of violence' (2001: 3). Other scholars have similarly argued for the impossibility of true objectivity in labelling violence. Nancy Armstrong and Leonard Tennenhouse write, 'To regard certain practices as violent is never to see them just as they are. It is always to take up a position for or against them' (1989: 9). Martin Barker argues even more specifically that the term 'violence' as we currently understand it emerged in the social context of the late 1950s and early 1960s as a response to social changes and political unrest, which underscores his crucial point that '"violence" is not an object which researchers have discovered, in the way that Australopithecus was discovered. "Violence" is an arbitrary re-labelling of behaviours, and then also of representations of those behaviours, which in its very act of naming achieves a number of political ends' (2004: 57).

If this is the case, then how do we decide what films should be considered 'violent'? One possible answer lies in a reception study of violent movies done by Annette Hill in which certain films were selected for study because their violent content 'exemplif[ied] societal/cultural consensus of extremely violent movies' (1997: 9). This is not to suggest that societal/cultural consensus is necessary to affix the 'violence' tag to a film, but rather to underscore the extremely subjective nature of such a label. Different cultures and generations construct their own definitions of film violence, so that a film that is deemed extraordinarily violent in one time or place may not be viewed as such elsewhere. There are numerous variables that play into this: the constantly fluctuating nature of film style and the appropriation and mainstreaming of innovative techniques (for example, the shocking quality of montage violence becoming the norm for action movies), the escalation of the graphic representation of bodily damage, changing styles of film acting (for example, overly theatrical death throes becoming inherently comical to later audiences), and the always evolving social and historical context in which a film is viewed.

The importance of this context can be seen in Vivian Sobchack's oft-reprinted 1974 article 'The Violent Dance: A Personal Memoir of Death in the Movies', in which she argues that the violent American films of the 1970s 'merely reflect our search for meaning and significance – for order – in the essentially senseless' (1976: 91). Her fundamental point is that the chaos and senselessness of real-life violence in American society in the 1970s directly influenced how she viewed and understood film violence at that time. Twenty years later, in an afterword to her original article, she notes that she no longer feels the same way. She ties her altered view of film violence to the change in the representations themselves: 'Violence on the screen and in the culture is not related to a moral context, but to a proliferation of images, texts, and spectacle' (2000: 124). However, she also connects this view with changes in her own personality and position in life: being a quarter of a century older and more in touch with her own mortality, Sobchack notes that 'I avoid violence in the movies because now, after various and intense experiences of physical pain, it affects me more strongly than it did before' (2000: 119).

Similarly, film violence that did not seem unnerving or particularly graphic in its original social/historical context can take on new intensity in hindsight. Harold Schechter (2005) offers a particularly pointed example in Disney's three-part *Davy Crockett* series, which originally aired as part of the *Disneyland* television series in 1954 and was then edited into a feature-length film and released theatrically in 1955 as *Davy Crockett, King of the Wild Frontier*. 'Mr. Disney has something here – for kids' wrote *New York Times* critic Bosley Crowther, who described the film as 'straight juvenile entertainment', all of which is 'okay' (1955: 36). The television series and the film were remarkably popular, leading to an onslaught of merchandising of which an estimated $300 million was sold. Yet, watching the film decades later and outside the context of Disney's 'disarming middlebrow didacticism', as Christopher Anderson puts it (1994: 144), Schechter found it to contain 'a staggering amount' of violence, so much so that he questions whether 'any kiddie programme today ... would permit the kinds of images that were transmitted to America's children by the Disney studio back in 1954 and embraced by the entire country as wholesome family entertainment' (2005: 24). Schechter notes scenes in which Davy Crockett (Fess Parker) and his sidekick Georgie Russell (Buddy Ebsen) slit one Indian guard's throat and stab another in the back; a lengthy clash at an Indian camp that results in a 'battleground littered with corpses'; and finally the Battle of the Alamo sequence, which he describes as having 'levels of carnage [that remain] unsurpassed in the history of televised children's entertainment' (2005: 25). While there is very little graphic bloodletting in these scenes, there is no doubt as to the penetration of bodies by knives, bayonets, swords, arrows and tomahawks. Yet, there is no record of any substantial complaints during the television series or the subsequent film release, perhaps because the focus of censorial attention was so squarely aimed at that time on crime and horror comic books, as well as television shows and movies featuring juvenile delinquency. Ensconced in a protective shield of history, mythology and nostalgia, Davy Crockett's violent exploits did not seem so dangerous, which suggests that, during the 1950s, moral reformers were much more concerned about the *content* of violent entertainment than its *style* (which will be discussed in detail later in the chapter).

Violence takes on a new intensity in hindsight: *Davy Crockett, King of the Wild Frontier* (1955)

Thus, film violence is best understood as a *perception*, a label that is affixed to cinematic representations of certain behaviours and actions. Film violence is an elastic, sliding, flexible term, one that shifts and changes throughout history and across various cultures. That which is defined as violent in one time or place may not be labelled as such in the future or in hindsight or in another culture. And, as Sobchack shows in her personal recollections of film violence during the 1970s and 1990s, the effect film violence has on an individual viewer can also shift across time and place. Different audiences view film violence differently, but even within the mind-set of the individual it is not a fixed entity and is always subject to reconsideration. Film violence is not one thing, but rather those actions and images that a viewer perceives as violent in a given time and place. It is, above all, an individual experience, which necessarily entails disagreement.

Components of film violence

Although we are defining film violence as a subjective experience, this does not let us off the ontological hook. In other words, this individualistic approach does not mean that there are no discernible factors that contribute to and help shape the perception of film violence. In fact, quite the opposite is true. There are a number of important elements that not only determine whether or not we call a visual or aural representation *violent*, but our specific responses to that violence. The subjective nature of our experiences dictates our relationship to these components, not the veracity of their existence.

Stephen Prince has focused much of his writing on the stylistic components of film violence. His working definition of film violence relies entirely on its ontological basis in representation. In one book he defines film violence as 'the stylistic encoding of a referential act' (2003: 34), and in a later article he defines it as 'a stylistic construction, a formal design that portrays an event on screen' (2006: 11). From this perspective, we can see film violence as having two primary components: the referential component (that is, the behaviour depicted) and the cinematic treatment (what Prince terms 'stylistic amplitude'), which is a function of graphicness and duration (2003: 35). To further expound on his stylistic focus, Prince (2003) presents a two-dimensional coordinate system to chart film violence: the referential component is on the *x*-axis and the stylistic design is on the *y*-axis.

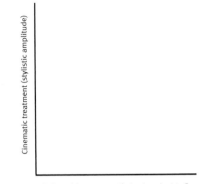

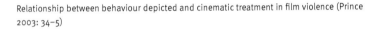

Referential component (behaviour depicted)

Relationship between behaviour depicted and cinematic treatment in film violence (Prince 2003: 34–5)

This model is particularly useful in charting the manner in which film violence has developed over the years, with the stylistic amplitude steadily increasing as filmmakers continue to load their aesthetic arsenals with new and innovative means of depicting bloodshed onscreen (particularly slow-motion, montage editing and special make-up effects) while the behaviour depicted has remained fairly consistent. This model also helps illustrate how, when viewers complain about the level of violence in the movies, they are usually talking about the stylistic amplitude, not the behaviours themselves, which marks a significant change from the early years of cinema when would-be censors were more concerned about the behaviours depicted (such as criminality). As we will see in the next chapter, people have been shooting and stabbing and slaughtering each other onscreen since the movies began, and the only difference between then and now is that filmmakers have adopted and made conventional increasingly graphic means of depicting these violent behaviours.

However, the balance of power between content and style can tip in both directions. It is commonplace to assume that style, especially in contemporary films, is the overriding component. However, some films can have virtually no onscreen gore, yet still be perceived as being explicitly violent. For example, Tobe Hooper's *The Texas Chain Saw Massacre* (1974) is often discussed as if it were graphically violent, when in fact very little blood is actually shed onscreen.[3] The actions in the film are no doubt horribly gruesome – a woman being hung alive on a meat hook while her dead boyfriend is dismembered on a table in front of her, a man in a wheelchair being sliced in half by a chainsaw – yet the presentation of these actions is surprisingly restrained given the film's grisly subject matter and attention-grabbing title. In fact, there is only one point in the entire film when we actually see a chainsaw meet flesh, and it is at the very end when Leatherface (Gunnar Hanson) drops the saw on his own leg and we see it cutting into him for a few seconds. Otherwise, the vast majority of the violence in this film is kept just offscreen in the same manner as classical Hollywood violence. It is the relentless nature of the violence – the nonstop presence of its threat – that makes the film seem so much more graphically violent than it is. It is a prime example of J. David Slocum's argument that 'the *threat* of harm or injury can often be as disturbing as the act itself' (2001: 2; emphasis in original). Similarly, Michael Powell's *Peeping Tom* was almost universally condemned during its initial release in Britain in 1960 due to its violent content. According to Carlos Clarens, '*Peeping Tom* was heavily censored in most countries; yet, in spite of its theme, the movie was far less gory than the most dignified of the Hammers. Critics and censors, united for once, seemed to find the display of terror more deplorable than actual blood-spilling' (1967: 146).

Any discussion of film style invariably brings up another important issue: whether or not we perceive film violence to be realistic. As numerous theorists have demonstrated (see Williams 1980), realism is a cinematic construct, a merging of stylistic devices with audience preconceptions to produce a sense in the individual viewer that what is being viewed is closely, if not exactly, analogous to their knowledge and experience of external reality. It is a given that realism as a concept is theoretically and practically complicated by all kinds of mediating factors, but violence complicates this even more because many, if not the majority of, viewers have never actually witnessed in real life the kind of violent actions that we routinely take for granted onscreen. We may perceive an image of a character being shot as realistic even if we have never actually seen someone shot in real life and therefore have no external criteria with which to make such a judgement. Paradoxically, the more stylistically enhanced the film violence is, the more realistic it often appears to audiences. For example, after a sneak preview of *The Wild Bunch* in 1969, viewers reported that Peckinpah's highly stylised used of slow-motion and montage editing had resulted in 'the most realistic motion picture yet conceived' (Prince 2006: 12). In a different vein, many viewers who are deeply disturbed by the impact of the violence in *Schindler's List* (1993) are probably unaware that the perceived realism of that film's atrocities are mediated largely by director Steven Spielberg's subtle use of documentary-like stylistic devices to close the distance between spectator and image. On the opposite end of the spectrum, if style becomes excessively marked, as it does in many contemporary action films such as *The Matrix* (1999), with its attention-grabbing 'bullet time' technique, it can ultimately distance the viewer from the impact of film violence, resulting in a giddy, pleasurable experience akin to a theme-park ride. When film violence is at its most powerful, it usually involves a finely balanced interaction between style and viewer expectations.

Because most of us have learned what violence 'looks like' through the media, for most viewers film violence is a purely self-referential image; that is, we recognise elements of violence onscreen largely in relation to other violent images we have seen in the movies and on television. As Joel Black notes, 'In today's film culture, our sense of what is real is determined, conditioned, and mediated as never before by movies and the other recording media' (2002a: 111). Stephen Prince offers a fascinating illustration of this in his case study of *The Passion of the Christ*. Prince shows that both critics and viewers perceive the film's treatment of the violence inflicted on Jesus's body to be rigorously and uncompromisingly realistic, but only because they have no frame of reference for judgement outside of previous Hollywood representations of the scourging and crucifixion that were less visually graphic and detailed.[4] Realism for these viewers 'is a function of what is most immediate and given to their perceptions' (2006: 21). Similarly, those who were raised since the 1960s when film violence became more regularly gruesome in Hollywood films – the era that mainstreamed 'the dirty reality of death – not suggestions but blood and holes', as Pauline Kael (1994: 149) put it – may have a hard time understanding why audiences were in any way disturbed by onscreen violence during the classical era, when characters were hit by bullets with no visual impact and died graceful, sometimes overly theatrical deaths.

However, beyond the visual and auditory encoding of the violence itself

More graphic than usual representations of the crucifixion: *The Passion of the Christ* (2004)

there are other crucial components that shape how violence is depicted and how the filmmaker intends for it to be received. Murray Pomerance suggests a taxonomy based on 'irony' and 'probability' as two discrete variables that help determine both the nature of film violence and how audiences understand it. Using these variables, he constructs a fourfold table for different types of screen violence: mechanical violence (probable and unironic; for example, *Star Wars* (1977)); mythic violence (probable and ironic; for example, *Commando* (1985)); idiomorphic violence (improbable and unironic; for example, *The Silence of the Lambs* (1991)); and dramaturgical violence (improbable and ironic; for example, the films of Alfred Hitchcock). Mechanical violence is the most typical kind of Hollywood violence, and 'its performance is framed in utterly conventional terms, fully reflecting expectations and stereotypes' (2004: 41). Mythic violence, on the other hand, 'attains a heightened status by contrast with a background in which violence – at least overt violence, oppression, repression, destruction – is not seen' (2004: 46). Idiomorphic violence is the opposite of mythic violence, presenting us with a 'distinct perpetrator' who is so evil that we 'often focus on the perpetrator rather than the circumstance' (ibid.). Finally, dramaturgical violence is the most difficult because it relies on both improbability and irony, and 'it intrigues and shocks because the irony of performance is delicate' (2004: 51).

Previously, Devin McKinney had offered a means of splitting film violence into a dichotomy of strong and weak. Strong violence 'often has the physical effects of the body genres', but 'also acts on the mind by refusing it glib comfort and immediate resolutions' (1993: 17). According to

McKinney, films characterised by strong violence include *Henry: Portrait of a Serial Killer* (1986), *The Crying Game* (1992) and *Bad Lieutenant* (1992). Weak violence, on the other hand, 'thrives on a sterile contradiction: it reduces bloodshed to its barest components, then inflates them with hot stylised air' (1993: 19). Films that employ weak violence include *Basic Instinct* (1992) and *Reservoir Dogs* (1992). Strong violence, therefore, finds a balance between style and content with the intention being to confront the viewer with the ugliness of violence, while weak violence has no content and is all style, with no intention other than to entertain and excite. Henry A. Giroux extends this logic by dividing film violence into three distinctions: ritualistic, hyper-real and symbolic violence. Ritualistic violence is the fuel that runs the action-adventure genre – 'the Arnold Schwarzenegger and Bruce Willis school of violence' (1996: 19), which is now most readily identified with the director Michael Bay. Such representations of violence 'derive their force' through repetition and serve to 'numb the senses with an endless stream of infantilised, histrionic flair' (1996: 61); it can be found in films such as *Die Hard* (1988) and *Speed* (1994), and more recently in films like *Bad Boys II* (2003) and *Wanted* (2008). Hyper-real violence, on the other hand, is marked by technology, irony and parody; it is found primarily in the films of Quentin Tarantino, most notably *Pulp Fiction*. Lastly, symbolic violence is, for Giroux, the most meaningful incarnation of filmic bloodshed, and it is found only in rare films such as *Platoon* (1986), *Unforgiven* (1992), *The Crying Game* and *Schindler's List*. Symbolic violence 'does not become an end in itself; it serves to reference a broader logic and set of insights' (1996: 62). In making such distinctions among arguably subjective types of film violence, scholars are grappling with a wide array of sometimes contradictory components that interact in multifaceted and often unintended ways to produce the *idea* of film violence.

In addition to the behaviours depicted and the stylistic encoding of those behaviours, there are many other components that are crucial to understanding any depiction of film violence. First, we must consider the *who*: who is enacting the violence and against whom? The very same violent behaviour will have extraordinarily different ramifications depending on who is enacting it. The who necessarily involves issues of spectatorship and identification. Most mainstream films use violence in ways that conform to social norms; that is, we are asked to deplore violence when it is used by villains or other characters deemed disreputable within the film's narrative and moral universe while at the same time we are asked to not only accept but applaud the use of violence when it is deployed by heroes or other 'good' characters. This disjunction is highlighted by the fact that many viewers get a jolt of exhilaration when a movie villain's violence is turned against him or her. For example, in *Rambo: First Blood Part II* (1985), the eponymous action hero (Sylvester Stallone) is captured by Soviet soldiers and tortured for information by being strapped to an electrified steel box-spring. The suffering that John Rambo endures under torture is clearly meant to both underscore his resolve and further vilify the sadistic villains. Yet, when Rambo eventually escapes, the film makes a point of showing him push one of his primary adversaries into the box-spring, after which he turns up the juice full throttle.

Another component that must be considered is the overall context in which the violence takes place. This is more than just the stylistic encoding of the violent act, but rather the tone and mood of both the violent scene and the film as a whole. The tone will suggest to the viewer, on both denotative and connotative levels, how the violence should be read. For example, viewers who would otherwise cringe at the sight of onscreen gore are still able to laugh during a sequence from *Monty Python and the Holy Grail* (1975) in which King Arthur (Graham Chapman) hacks off the arms and legs of his adversary, the Black Knight (John Cleese). The violence in

The tone with which this gory maiming is presented shapes the audience's response: *Monty Python and the Holy Grail* (1975)

this scene is depicted with slightly shoddy effects that nonetheless make full use of squirting arteries and shredded tissue. While this can make for effective comedy, coupling strong violence with a tone that might be perceived as 'inappropriate' is a frequent point of criticism, especially for contemporary Hollywood films that have effectively mixed comedy and realistic violence (see King 2004). Henry A. Giroux has been particularly critical of how representations of violence in contemporary Hollywood cinema have been a major factor in the re-emergence of a new kind of racism, reactionary politics, cynicism and an erasure of important social realities: 'the reality of everyday violence is supplemented by a culture of violence produced as entertainment' (1996: 65).

Thus, as we have seen, there are numerous components that help to shape our perception of violence on the screen. The behaviour itself must be considered, as well as the stylistic manner in which it is depicted. We must also give thought to the realism of the film violence, which is directly related to both the behavioural and stylistic components, as well as audience expectations. Furthermore, there are fundamental narrative issues that shape our perceptions, such as who is enacting the violence and why, as well as the overall tone of the scene and the film as a whole. Therefore, it is not difficult to see why talking about film violence is such a complex and controversial issue, which leads us to the question: how is film violence discursively constructed?

The history of the film violence idea

In the opening pages of *More Than Night: Film Noir in Its Contexts*, James Naremore asserts that film noir – as a category, as a genre, as a cycle, as a style – is ultimately impossible to organise in any satisfactory way. Sidestepping the decades-old debates about what film noir ultimately is, Naremore instead argues that the concept of film noir 'has less to do with a group of artifacts than with a discourse – a loose, evolving system of arguments and readings that helps to shape commercial strategies and aesthetic ideologies' (1998: 11).

Something quite similar can be said about film violence. We have already dispelled the notion that film violence is some 'thing', and another means of looking at the concept is to consider how it has been discussed over the years – to, in effect, map the scholarly, political and popular discourse surrounding film violence to see how it has been defined by those who have some stake in its conception. Because film violence is a construct – seemingly obvious, but always shifting and slipping – we should examine the various ways in which it has been constructed since the dawn of cinema.

The study of screen violence dates back to the beginnings of the medium itself, although it was not until the late 1960s that a significant number of scholars began to seriously consider film violence outside of an empirical effects frame of research. The dominance of empirical effects methodologies in the discourse around film violence is due to both the continual anxieties among the general public about the potential negative effects of viewing mediated violence, especially on children's social and emotional development, and the ease with which this topic is co-opted by politicians and other public figures to illustrate what many view as the moral decay of contemporary culture. However, notable advancements have been made in recent years to reconceptualise film violence as a complex signifying practice within specific historical moments in a way that greatly complicates any essentialist notions of how mediated violence functions in society.

In the first half of the twentieth century prior, to the institutionalisation of film studies as a liberal arts academic discipline, the study of motion pictures in America was largely confined to a body of empirical research that sought to connect the influence of watching movies to negative behaviours, ranging from juvenile delinquency, to casual sexuality, to the spread of socialism.[5] This empirical focus on behavioural effects culminated in the 13 studies published between 1933 and 1936 known as the Payne Fund Studies. The findings of these studies, which were conducted nationwide between 1929 and 1933, were summarised for popular consumption in Henry James Forman's *Our Movie Made Children* (1933). Although the Payne Fund Studies themselves resulted in mostly contradictory findings and, to a certain extent, dismantled myths about the movies' excessive influence over viewers, Forman's book was written with the clear intention of arguing that the movie industry needed to be regulated; thus, he focused heavily on the findings that suggested harmful effects (see Jowett 1971: 71). A simple overview of his chapter titles makes this obvious, with 'Molded by the Movies' and 'Movie-Made Criminals' leaving no doubt in the reader's mind that viewing movies can have a direct, formative influence over a child's cognitive and moral development. At one point, he writes:

> If a motion picture can change sympathies and attitudes and affect conduct, it becomes of enormous importance as a factor in our education, in our standards, in all the social fabric of our lives. So important does it become, that if it did not exist, we should incontinently desire to invent it; and so significant that if it falls short of the best and highest quality attainable, the entire country should feel instantly moved to eradicate whatever defects it carries, in view of its influences upon the young, and to make it, as nearly as human agency can, perfect. (1933: 122)

That paragraph is a perfect distillation of how many people viewed motion pictures and why it was deemed necessary to institute 'corrective' measures such as the Hollywood studio-enforced Production Code to 'eradicate' (or at least minimise and control) such 'defects' as sex and violence. Although neither the Payne Fund Studies nor *Our Movie Made Children* focused primarily on issues of film violence, they successfully established the requisite 'scientific validity' to justify common sense fears about the harmful effects movies have on the moral and social well-being of their viewers, and it is in this position that much of the debate about film violence has been couched ever since.

Articles and research on film violence simmered throughout the 1940s, 1950s and early 1960s. During this time, the enforcement of the Production Code in Hollywood cinema restricted graphic depictions of violence onscreen; the moral indignation of reform-minded groups focused instead on the new bearer of social ills, broadcast television, as well as comic books[6]; and the general public consciousness was enraptured by Senator Joseph McCarthy's very public communist witch hunt.

During this time, some researchers began to challenge the negative social effects model by investigating the theory of emotional catharsis through viewing violence onscreen. Much of the early scientific thinking about catharsis theory stemmed from energy models of motivation, which suggested that many different kinds of activities, including fantasy and competitive sports, help reduce a person's inclinations to act aggressively towards others. The most frequently cited experiment supporting the catharsis, or drive-reduction, theory was performed by Seymour Feshbach, in which he concluded that 'fantasy behaviour is an adjustment mecha-nism which can serve to reduce tensions and provide substitute goal satis-factions. It may function as an outlet for socially unacceptable motives and frustrated achievement strivings' (1955: 10). However, conflicting results in later studies meant that the catharsis theory was never given any substan-tial empirical support; thus, the idea of violent entertainment stimulating violent behaviour remained the dominant discourse.

This only increased with the eventual dismantling of the Production Code and the institution of the Motion Picture Association of America's (MPAA) ratings system in 1968, which greatly expanded filmmakers' free-dom to depict violence in more graphic terms. The result was renewed inter-est in the screen violence debate, and Congressional enquiries into the effects of violence in both the movies and on television in the 1960s led to several large-scale research projects, including *Mass Media and Violence: A Report to the National Commission on the Causes and Prevention of Violence* (Lange, Baker & Ball 1969) and *Television and Growing Up: The Impact of Televised Violence* (Cisin *et al.* 1972).

At the same time, there was an outpouring of articles in the popular press decrying what was perceived as steadily increasing levels of graphic violence onscreen. In a 1967 article in *Reader's Digest*, Senator Margaret Chase Smith noted how offended she was that 'boys and girls today are increasingly exposed to such sick violence for the sake of the quarters and dollars they contribute to America's $3-billion-a-year motion-picture industry' (1967: 139). In her brief article, Smith dismissed the catharsis theory, condemned Hollywood for 'urging' children to see 'sex, violence, and sadism in theatres from coast to coast' (ibid.), and supported her argument with quotes from Leonard Berkowitz, a psychologist at the University of Wisconsin, and Frederic Wertham, the psychologist best known for *Seduction of the Innocent* (1954), his alarmist book about the unseemly influence of horror and crime comic books.[7] But, it was not just senators and moral reform groups who were vocal in their criticism of the new violence of the late 1960s. Established film critics also voiced their disgust, most notably Bosley Crowther of the *New York Times*, who, in a now infamous review that was the perfect distillation of the generation gap in 1967, called *Bonnie and Clyde* 'a cheap piece of bald-faced slapstick comedy' in which 'the blending of farce with brutal killings is as point-less as it is lacking in taste' (1967b: 36). Crowther was one of the most vocal critics of violence in the movies, at one point arguing that violence is nothing less than 'antisocial venom': 'It is the fallacious idea that violent movies are playing an important cultural role as ironic reflection and commentators on these sad events are offering release for anxieties and torn emotions with their excessive fantasies that some thoughtful critics and philosophers use to rationalise their end' (1967a: 69).

However, at this same time, several scholars were breaking out of conventional moulds and beginning to analyse film violence using textual strategies to tease out social and political implications that were ignored by the statistics-driven, content-analysis approaches employed by empirical effects research. This period of research in the late 1960s and early 1970s is considered 'the golden age' of both violence in American films and its study (see Slocum 2001: 7). One of the first sustained efforts to study violent American films cast its analysis into the then-recent past. Published in 1971 as a companion book to a series of films exhibited at the Museum of Modern Art in New York from 24 April to 6 June 1969, Lawrence Alloway's *Violent America: The Movies 1946–1964* established much of the foundation on which future studies of film violence could be constructed. On one level, it is somewhat ironic that Alloway's book, published during the 'golden age' of American film violence, did not take any of those contemporaneous films into account. However, its treatment of primarily mainstream action films from Hollywood studios that were released roughly between the court-enforced break-up of the studio system that began in the late 1940s, and the final death throes of the Production Code in the late 1960s, aptly shows how the depiction of graphic film violence was steadily increasing during these tumultuous years, thus serving as a lead-in to the bloody balletics of *Bonnie and Clyde* and calling into question why critics like Bosley Crowther were at all surprised at the development.

Alloway's goal was to study 'the transformations of meaning undergone by set figures and set situations, revealed by the forms of movie violence under the pressure of the contemporary world' (1971: 7). Thus, his approach to studying film violence established two significant arguments that would be followed by other humanistic scholars attempting to move out of the empirical effects framework: (1) film violence is a signifying practice that has evolved and continues to evolve over time; and (2) depictions of violence are linked, both directly and indirectly, with the socio-cultural climate in which they are created. For instance, Alloway links the 1950s cycle of 'weapon westerns', which focused on the power and social impact of new weapons in the late nineteenth century, to 'the effect in audiences of veterans who had handled guns in World War Two and in Korea' (1971: 39). Similarly, he attributes 'the increased visibility of wounds' in movies of the 1960s to reports about casualties in Vietnam, an argument also made by Stephen Prince (1998, 2000a) and David A. Cook (1999) in discussing the development of the use of squibs to depict bullet wounds in the late-1960s films of Arthur Penn and Sam Peckinpah. As Alloway states rather bluntly, 'The level of information that is available in the other media is bound to have its analogues in the topical medium of film' (1971: 39).

The last chapter of Alloway's book is devoted solely to moralistic critiques and the empirical analysis of film violence. While he thoroughly dispenses with any notion that violent movies offer a cathartic release, Alloway also offers serious reservations about the then-current state of empirical effects research, arguing that 'What is needed in media research is first a contextual view of the experiences of representative members of the audience, and second a critical approach that does not break the continuities with earlier research' (1971: 68). Thus, Alloway essentially argues for research into film violence based on a combination of experimental psychology and media sociology, which means that, despite his broadening the study of film violence by including sociological analysis, genre theory and textual criticism, he still eventually reverts to a social-scientific frame.

Three years later, John Fraser's *Violence in the Arts* marked a major step forward in the humanistic analysis of film violence. While his book does not deal exclusively with films, it is important for the study of film violence because he completely avoids framing his study within effects research, deeming it 'bedeviled by excessive responsiveness to plot and insufficient alertness to the range and variety of conventions that are often involved' (1974: 8). Fraser's major contribution to the discourse on film violence is his manner of complicating both the depictions of violence and our responses to them. Borrowing a phrase from D. H. Lawrence, he emphasises that his primary interests are 'the ways in which ... "our sympathies flow and recoil" in our dealings with violence in the arts, and ... why some violences seem to make for intellectual clarity and a more civilised consciousness, while others make for confusion' (1974: ix). It is precisely Fraser's emphasis on the polysemous nature of violence that had been lacking in most writing about the subject prior to the late 1960s, and Fraser's provocative assertion that violence could lead to 'intellectual clarity and a more civilised consciousness' is something of a revolutionary statement in and of itself (it reads as a direct response to Bosley Crowther's dismissal of the 'fallacious' idea that screen violence could play 'an important cultural role' (1967a: 69)). Fraser's analysis spans across media and genres, real and recreated violence, illustrating how it is all articulated together in a variety of complex ways. While his book is short and remains primarily on a meta-analytic level, it offers one of the first and most striking examples of how to complicate thinking about depictions of violence.

Around this same time, several short, semi-academic books with plenty of ghastly full-page photographs were published to cash in on the popularity of film violence. One of them, Rick Trader Witcombe's *Savage Cinema*, does not offer a substantial or groundbreaking analysis of film violence, but it does function as a useful summary of the evolution of film violence up until the time of its publication. Witcombe's thesis is that 'To a far greater extent than television or theatre, [film] is about the texture of violence in modern living. It is almost true to say that on one level or another, movies deal with nothing but violence in its assorted forms' (1975: 7). The totalising effect of this statement is certainly debatable, but the notion that violence is one of the most persistent subjects explored by all movies is certainly one that bears further consideration, especially as it relates to what literary theory has recognised for a long time, namely that the basis of all drama is conflict, a form of violence. *Savage Cinema* is typical of the sociological influence on film studies in the 1970s, as Witcombe asserts that 'It can be said that violence in the cinema is merely a reflection of violence in society' (1975: 11) and 'Each age throws up its own type of violent movie, its own genre' (1975: 41). He also employs the often-used, but questionable argument that, in an ordered, modern society in which we are insulated from the ugliness and violence of life and death that used to be part of the texture of life, graphic violence in the cinema is somehow a sociological and psychological necessity. Witcombe refers to this as a 'Dionysian compensation',[8] which also includes arena sports: 'Savage cinema represents the Dionysius Factor in modern life, committed to restoring the atayisms [*sic*], blood-lust and aggression, love of the victor, contempt for the vanquished' (1975: 11). This particular idea has also been articulated by director Martin Scorsese, who has suggested that 'Maybe we need the catharsis of bloodletting and decapitation like the ancient Romans needed it, as ritual but not real like the Roman circus' (quoted in Plagens *et al.* 1991: 48).

In 1976, the Monarch Film Studies series published *Graphic Violence on the Screen*, a thin volume edited by Thomas R. Atkins, containing an introduction and five essays loosely organised around genres notable for their displays of violence: film noir, British horror films produced by Hammer Film Studios, Italian spaghetti westerns, kung fu films and modern low-budget horror films, whose chief representative was *The Texas Chain Saw Massacre*. This volume also contains Vivian Sobchack's aforementioned essay 'The Violent Dance: A Personal Memoir of Death in the Movies', in which she offers a psychological need for screen violence that differs from Witcombe's 'Dionysian compensation'. As noted earlier in this chapter, Sobchack relates onscreen violence to the fear felt by many in her generation as a result of the violence of the late 1960s: 'Death by violence became a possibility for all of us because it lacked sense and meaning much of the time; there was no drama and catharsis' (1976: 83). In a way, aestheticised violence onscreen both reflected the social chaos of the 1960s and also gave it a kind of order and meaning that was otherwise lacking. Thus, Sobchack argues, it was this fear of, and desire to make sense of, senseless death that drove viewers – even those who did not 'enjoy' watching film violence – to stare at the screen, wide-eyed, as Sobchack did when viewing Sam Peckinpah's *Straw Dogs* (1971):

> Fear has made even the most squeamish of us take our hands from our eyes. We are still afraid of violence and blood and death, but we are more afraid of the unknown – particularly when it threatens us personally and immediately. Even those of us who couldn't stand the sight of blood at one time find our desire to know and understand blood stronger than our desire not to see what frightens and sickens us. (1976: 87).

Sobchack's psychological rationalisation of the need to view violence in order to know the unknowable may strike some as too personal an explanation, but it does have a certain draw, especially in the current information age that is defined as much by conspiracy theories of with-held information (often about violence; for example, the Kennedy assassination, civilian atrocities in Vietnam, actual numbers of people killed in the Gulf War, the real causes of the 9/11 attacks and so on) as it is by the free flow of information through new channels and technologies. The psychology of the appeal of mediated violence is a complex topic, but surprisingly, it has been paid little attention by clinical psychologists and other researchers.[9]

There was not a substantial amount of writing about film violence throughout the 1980s outside of continued effects research. As it had been before the late 1960s, film violence receded to the academic background, becoming more of a secondary concern in screen studies, analysed only in terms of how it functioned in relation to another area of study. Rarely was it the primary focus of analysis. So, for instance, uses of film violence were raised several times in the work of Susan Jeffords (1989, 1994), but only in relation to Hollywood's themes of masculinity. In discussing the body of John Rambo as a performative display of aesthetic technology (linked specifically to the eroticising of technology and weapons), Jeffords asserts that violence is used in the *Rambo* films as a means to de-eroticise Rambo's body: 'the chief mechanism in mainstream cinema for deferring eroticism in the heterosexual male body is through establishing that body as an object of violence, so that erotic desire can be displaced as sado-masochism' (1989: 13).[10] Thus, the uses of violence in spectacle action films of the 1980s are not viewed as particularly important in and of them-selves, but only in how they function in relation to Reagan-era tropes of asserting heterosexual masculinity. However, Jeffords' explanations about how spectacles of death and war are eroticised and aestheticised to the point of becoming '"pure" moments in themselves that do not need to be contextualised or interpreted, simply witnessed, in order to be controlled' (1989: 10) prefigures the approach taken towards film violence by most scholars in the late 1990s.

The 1990s witnessed the evolution of what has been termed 'new' or 'ironic' violence in the films of such directors as Quentin Tarantino, Paul Verhoeven, Tony Scott, John Woo and Oliver Stone, and it was not long before there was a resurgence in scholarship on film violence that both examined this 'new violence' and also put it into context with previous forms of violent cinema. Several collections of essays on the topic were published at this time, including *Screen Violence* (French 1996), *Why We Watch: The Attractions of Violent Entertainment* (Goldstein 1998), *Screening Violence* (Prince 2000b), *Violence and American Cinema* (Slocum 2001) and *New Hollywood Violence* (Schneider 2004), as well as general surveys of violent cinema such as Stephen Hunter's *Violent Screen* (1995), which collects the *Baltimore Sun* critic's reviews of violent films from 1982–95; Laurent Bouzereau's *Ultraviolent Movies* (1996), which covers the well-worn ground from the late 1960s (epitomised by Sam Peckinpah) to the mid-1990s (epitomised by Quentin Tarantino); and Jake Horsley's *The Blood Poets* (1999a, 1999b), an ambitiously extensive, two-volume survey of violent films from 1958–99.

While desiring to continue the work begun by scholars of the early 1970s to complicate film violence as a signifying practice, much of this scholarship has succeeded primarily in setting up a binary between film violence of the 1970s, which is seen as complex and socially meaningful, and film violence of the 1990s, which is more explicit, but also more simplistic and socially meaningless. For example, at the end of *Savage Cinema*, his detailed historical/aesthetic study of Sam Peckinpah, Stephen Prince argues that Peckinpah's legacy has been hijacked by postmodern filmmakers who employ his aesthetic techniques for the purposes of vicarious excitement, thus removing them 'from the contexts in his work that gave them meaning', which renders them 'superficial and mechanical' (1998: 230). Of course, Prince is hardly alone in the assertion that filmic violence has lost much of its impact. In her afterword to 'The Violent Dance', Vivian Sobchack also bemoans the use of violence in contemporary films, arguing that it no longer functions as a means to help the viewer give order to social chaos: 'Today, most American films have more interest in the presence of violence than in its meaning' (2000: 120). Sobchack relates this partially to the change in American culture since the 1960s, as we are now living in a time when '"Senseless" or "random" violence … is barely remarkable or specific any longer' (2000: 123). However, the primary critique is that filmmakers have become 'careless' with their use of violence. Similarly, according to Devin McKinney, 'Over the past few years a new ethos of violence has been accruing in the commercial cinema; directors have been attempting to take it further – but not necessarily deeper' (1993: 16). On that same note, Henry A. Giroux has charged that 'Violence has become increasingly a source of pleasure', primarily as 'a site of voyeuristic titillation and gory spectacle' (1996: 58).

The idea of film violence being 'pleasurable' has always been a controversial idea, despite the fact that millions of ticket buyers around the world consistently suggest that it is. This is the essentially contradictory nature of film violence: the only thing louder than the condemnations of film violence is the accumulated sound of viewers stampeding to the next violent film, whether it is some variant of action spectacle like *The Dark Knight* and *Transformers: Revenge of the Fallen* (2009) or a gory horror film like the recent remakes of *The Texas Chainsaw Massacre* (2003) and *Friday the 13th* (2009). While film violence has been demonised as morally corrupt and pathologised as a societal sickness to be eradicated, there still persists the notion that it can play a meaningful, constructive role in society outside of moral or aesthetic corruption. As novelist Poppy Z. Brite notes:

> The poetry of violence is loathed by many and denied by even more. Violence cannot encompass beauty, claim these squeamish souls; by its very nature violence is crude, base, evil, and nothing but. Those of us who savour it, even on paper or film, are probably evil, too: we've surrendered our very humanity for a peek at someone's innards. (1996: 63–4)

However, as Brite also notes, not all mediated violence is equal, and not all of it should be used in the same way. But, even in allowing that conceit, there is still the problem of convincing those 'squeamish souls' that mediated violence has any role at all to play in society outside of general depravity. This is a difficult project, and even those who have written thoughtfully about, and admitted their own taste for, mediated violence have had trouble divorcing its seemingly inherent sordidness from any useful social role it might play.

To summarise, we have seen how film violence is not a single 'thing', but rather a complex set of signifying practices that are above all understood by viewers as a subjective experience. Film violence is both behaviour and style, and it is informed on all levels – from conception to reception – by the socio-historical context in which it is created, the aesthetic impulses of the filmmaker, pressures from external regulations and the mood and tenor of the audience who views it. Despite several common, fundamental components, film violence is best understood as a *perception* that is used to label represented behaviours and actions. It is an elastic, sliding, flexible term that has shifted and changed throughout history and across various cultures, and it continues to do so. In the next chapter, we will examine a brief history of film violence, which will illustrate both consistencies and significant variations in how violent behaviours have been depicted onscreen and how they have been understood by audiences.

2   A HISTORY OF FILM VIOLENCE

> The Cinématographe [is] the main attraction of the season ... [It will
> bring to the screen] bullfights, beheadings in China, atrocities in
> Armenia, and lynchings in Texas, some people are going to make
> barrels of money.
>
> *Phonoscope*, November 1896 (quoted in Spehr 2001: 20)

> Violence is one of the greatest things you can do in cinema. Edison
> invented the camera to *do* violence, all right?
>
> Quentin Tarantino, justifying his use of violence in
> *Reservoir Dogs* (quoted in Biskind 2004: 120)

The cinema is inherently violent; as a medium it is best suited to depicting violence. As J. David Slocum notes, 'From the technical nature of the
medium itself to the pleasures and anxieties it evokes in viewers, from its
layered narratives to frequently graphic spectacles, cinema is thoroughly
violent – even as that violence is difficult to explain simply' (2001: 4).
According to Jake Horsley, 'Cinema, from its very first moments, was, like
a blow to the retina that broke right through to the brain, an intrinsically
aggressive, assault[ing], and *violent* medium' (1999a: xxxvi; emphasis in
original). Similarly, Stephen Prince suggests that the appeal of film violence 'is tied to the medium's inherent visceral properties' (2000a: 2). He
also views violence 'as an essential component of cinema: part of its deep

formal structure, something that many filmmakers have been inherently drawn toward and something that cinema does supremely well' (2003: 3). Many film scholars and historians have noted that violence has been a part of the cinema since its earliest days; Erwin Panofsky argues that part of the development of motion pictures from simple recordings of movement to genuine visual art was their incorporation of 'a primordial instinct for bloodshed and cruelty' (1951: 754). However, the relationship between film and violence has even deeper roots than simply the content of the earliest movies.

The first true motion-picture camera, the Kinetograph, was created and tested in the West Orange, New Jersey laboratories of Thomas Alva Edison around 1891. At the same time, Edison was involved in the development of the electric utility industry, which was a direct outgrowth of his having perfected the electric incandescent light bulb in 1879. Throughout the 1880s Edison was engaged in a lengthy battle with George Westinghouse and Nikola Tesla over how electric power would be distributed: via Edison's direct current (DC) system or via Westinghouse's alternating current (AC) system. In a bid to undermine his opponents, Edison enacted a massive propaganda campaign to show that AC current was literally dangerous, which resulted in his demonstrating said lethal nature by using AC current to publicly electrocute dogs and cats. This practice culminated in one of Edison's grandest and most gruesome publicity stunts, in which he personally arranged for the use of alternating current to execute Topsy, a three-ton Coney Island elephant that had killed three men in as many years. The event, which was recorded in breathless detail in the following day's *New York Times*, was also filmed by Edison's motion picture company and released as *Electrocuting an Elephant* (1903).

During this time, Edison was instrumental in the development of the electric chair's use of AC current as a means of state execution, and he argued that the process should be referred to as 'Westinghousing', rather than 'electrocution'. Thus, there was a strange parallel between the invention of motion pictures and the invention of the electric chair, which is further underscored by the frequent appearance of the latter in the early days of the former. When the anarchist Leon Czolgosz was electrocuted in Auburn Prison on 29 October 1901, for the assassination of President William McKinley, an early movie theatre owner offered $2,000 for the rights to film the condemned man walking into the death chamber (see

Brandon 1999: 213). The movie theatre owner was apparently denied this right, but Edison, always ready to capitalise, had the event recreated in precise detail for his cameras, which he released a week and a half later as *Execution of Czolgosz, With Panorama of Auburn Prison* (1901).

The simultaneity of the fundamentally modern developments of motion pictures and the lethal use of electricity by the same publicity-seeking inventor might be dismissed as mere historical coincidence, but what cannot be dismissed is the frequently violent content of so many early motion pictures. As Charles Musser asserts, 'Sex and violence figured prominently in American motion pictures from the outset' (1990: 78), which he suggests is due to the fact that the individualised nature of early peepshow machines like Edison's Kinetoscope encouraged such images that would otherwise offend 'polite society'. However, the prevalence of the appeal of violence in early cinema does not suggest a monolithic audience. Rather, the audiences for early cinema cut across class divides, drawing from working, middle and elite classes, all of whom apparently desired on some level – conscious or subconscious – to see violence both enacted and re-enacted.

Violence in the silent era

From the first flickerings of moving images in individual peepshow machines, to the projections on the walls of tiny storefront theatres, the cinema has always been fascinated by images of brutality. The brief, one-minute actualities of early movie history (1880s and 1890s) are often thought of fondly as the charming, nostalgic capturing on celluloid of simpler times; one's mind might immediately recall the innocent imagery of Louis and Auguste Lumière's *Repas de bébé* (*The Baby's Meal*, 1895) or *L'arroseur arrosé* (*The Sprinkler Sprinkled*, 1895), or even Thomas Edison's then-scandalous *The Kiss* (1896). While these and many other such films captured street scenes, family life and images of natural beauty, there were many others that focused on boxing matches, cock fights, bull fights, terriers attacking rats, fires and natural disasters. While it would take nearly 15 years for filmmakers to fully develop the cinematic language of narrative to spin violent tales, the camera lenses of the first filmmakers were immediately drawn to violence, chaos and destruction, both natural and human-made.

In particular, films of prizefights, both actual and re-enacted, were among the most popular of early cinematic attractions and even helped to influence the development of the medium itself: although Edison had mentioned prizefights as a potential subject, they were not initially filmed because the Kinetograph camera and corresponding Kinetoscope exhibition device could only hold a maximum of fifty feet of film, which would provide twenty to forty seconds of recording and playback depending on the rate of exposure. Otway Latham, who along with his father, brother and a college friend started a film exhibition company in 1894, solved this problem by extending both machines' capacity for film to 150 feet and slowing down the rate of exposure to thirty frames per second (instead of the typical forty fps). This increased the running time to just over a minute, which was roughly the length of a single round of boxing (see Musser 1990: 82). The Lathams began to stage bouts between well-known pugilists for the camera (the first being between Michael Leonard and Jack Cushing on 14 June 1894), which were covered by the newspapers and drew strong crowds at the Kinetoscope parlours. From 1894 to 1915, approximately one hundred boxing films were made, most of which were produced by the largest and most successful film companies, including the Edison Company, whose *Corbett and Courtney Before the Kinetograph* (1894) was one of its most consistently popular films (see Streible 1989: 236).

Prizefighting had been criminalised in virtually every state in the Union by 1896, thus watching filmed accounts of the fights or staged recreations was often the only avenue for people to see the popular bloodsport. The films themselves were immensely popular, especially the heavyweight title bouts, which could fill gala premiers at legitimate New York City theatres (see Streible 1989). Thus, the popularity of prizefight films was a crucial early moment in the history of film violence because it established the nascent medium's role in allowing audiences to experience vicariously that which they were denied in their everyday lives. In this regard, prizefight films provided the fundamental template for engaging with film violence long before the development of both narrative and formal elements like editing and camera movement.

Not surprisingly, such films were quickly targeted by moral reform groups and censorious legislators who were as eager to protect the public from the barbarity of fistic violence on film as they were in person. While an 1897 House bill aimed at criminalising pictures and descriptions of prizefights failed to pass, numerous states enacted similar legislation. The pressure on prizefight films began to wane over the next few years as the sport became more legitimate in the public eye, but it picked up again in 1909 following the appearance of a fight film depicting the defeat of heavyweight champion Tommy Burns by the African-American fighter John Arthur 'Jack' Johnson. The censoring of all subsequent Jack Johnson films is an important early illustration of how the moral panic around images of violence is frequently conflated with other social concerns, in this case the increasing threat to the widespread belief in white superiority. As Dan Streible writes, 'Although outlawing the violent brutality of boxing may have been a true concern for some, it was also a subterfuge for others who wished to curtail the presence of an imposing, powerful black figure and the inspirational effect he could have for black America' (1989: 248).

Another of the favoured subjects of early motion pictures was the recreation of violent historical events. Beheadings, in particular, were a popular subject for many years because of the sensational nature of the action and also because this subject allowed filmmakers to display their virtuosity with early special effects. The most famous of these is the Edison Company's 1894 Kinetoscope film *The Execution of Mary, Queen of Scots*, whose title promises a grisly spectacle created just for the camera. The film is important in the history of the cinema because it employed one of the first cinematic special effects, 'stop-motion substitution', which allowed the filmmaker to have an actor playing Mary (in this case, the Edison Company's secretary and treasurer Robert Thomae) kneel down in front of the executioner's block, after which he could stop the camera and then substitute a dummy whose head was then hacked off (the head rolls off the block and a witness picks it up and holds it aloft to ensure maximum effect). Because no one else in the shot moved during the switch, to the viewer it appears to be one continuous action caught in a single shot, which enhances the perceived realism of the beheading. While this film recreates a recorded historical incident, its lurid appeal to sensationalised violence is undeniable, making it a primitive precursor to the 'don't look away' shock of the razor-to-the-eyeball scene in Luis Buñuel and Salvador Dalí's *Un chien andalou* (1929). Or, as Harold Schechter aptly describes it, 'a mini-splatter movie, designed to provide morbid titillation under the usual guise of cultural edification' (2005: 113).

The Edison Company's grisly cinematic innovation was emulated by others, particularly film pioneer Sigmund Lubin, who used the Boxer Rebellion (1899–1901) in China as an excuse to produce re-enactments of Chinese atrocities under such titles as *Chinese Massacring Christians* (1900) and *Beheading of a Chinese Prisoner* (1900). Georges Méliès, who is generally considered the father of cinematic special effects, also had a fondness for beheadings, in both fantasy-comedies such as *Le bourreau turc* (*The Terrible Turkish Executioner*, 1904), in which an executioner lops off four prisoners' heads at once, after which the prisoners reattach their heads and then cut the executioner in half with his own scimitar, and in historical recreations such as *Les Derniers moments d'Anne de Boleyn* (aka *The Tower of London,* 1905). And, if clever recreations were not intense enough, many Kinetoscope machines played loops of newsreel footage of actual atrocities, including the beheadings of six men accused of being bandits by the Chinese army outside Mukden, the guillotining of four French criminals at Bethune (which led to the first instance of French film censorship in 1909), and the hanging of a cattle rustler in Missouri (see Mathews 1994: 9–10; Philips 1975: 14). According to Joel Black, 'In the early years of cinema, scenes of actual death were as likely to be encountered as their simulations' (2002b: 64).

Many film historians have argued that the Spanish-American War in 1898, which was the first war to be documented by motion picture cameras, literally saved the medium by redefining its potential from cheap novelty to journalistic enterprise. Nevertheless, while the majority of the films made around this time were actualities of battleships and marching troops, filmmakers could not resist the urge to recreate battle scenes and atrocities for the camera, most likely as a ploy to depict the 'savagery' of the Spanish and thus support American involvement in the war. Two examples from 1898 are *Cuban Ambush* and *Shooting Captured Insurgents*, both of which were produced by the Edison Company. While *Cuban Ambush* is a relatively unremarkable re-enactment of Cuban forces firing at a Spanish scouting party from the windows of an old fort, *Shooting Captured Insurgents* is something entirely different. Obviously shot in the same location as *Cuban Ambush*, it depicts a regiment of Spanish soldiers marching captured insurgents to the wall of the fort, lining them up face forward, stepping back and then executing them with close-range rifle volley. While not explicit in terms of blood and gore, *Shooting Captured*

Insurgents is a surprisingly disturbing forty seconds of cinema not only because it so closely approximates a documentary view of an actual event (like Lubin's atrocity films of the Boxer Rebellion, it lacks the historical distance of *The Execution of Mary, Queen of Scots*), but because the violence is so brutal and uncompromising. That is, there is no conventional action excitement to be found, only the cold, hard image of execution.

While Geoff King (2004) argues that the mixing of comedy and explicit violence is a specific commercial strategy of the New Hollywood, there are numerous antecedents in the earliest days of silent cinema. There is Méliès' aforementioned *The Terrible Turkish Executioner*, for example, as well as Cecil Hepworth's *Explosion of a Motor Car* (1900), which depicts a car riding down a quaint suburban street and then suddenly, inexplicably exploding. The film's gag, however, is revealed when a policeman walks over to inspect the remains of the car, only to be battered with the dismembered bodies of the ill-fated passengers, which come raining out of the sky after a comically extended period of time. Despite the lack of blood and patent fakery of the severed limbs, the film's attempt to get laughs from the explosive dismemberment of multiple innocents is still surprisingly shocking.

As filmmakers in the early silent era began to experiment with rudimentary storytelling frameworks, they also began to incorporate violence as a narrative strategy while refining the effects used to depict it onscreen. The recreation of famous crimes and criminal activities found great popularity on the screen, just as they had in so-called 'Penny Dreadfuls' and in various ballads about crime and executions during the nineteenth century. Edwin S. Porter's prototypical blockbuster *The Great Train Robbery* (1903) is a telling example of the importance of the thrill of violent criminal action to early audiences. Although tame by today's standards, largely because of the lack of blood and the performers' dated acting style, the violence in *The Great Train Robbery* is nonetheless quite malicious, including a robber shooting a fleeing civilian in the back, another robber beating a man atop the moving train and then throwing his lifeless body off the side, and the eventual gunning down of the criminals by a band of rangers. The film is also important for the way that Porter plays with violence and audience identification. As Charles Musser argues, the infamous emblematic shot that features actor Justus D. Barnes, who played one of the robbers, firing his six-shooter directly into the camera 'added realism … by intensifying the spectators' identification with the victimised travellers' (1990: 354–55). In early cinema, emblematic shots, which could be placed at either the beginning or end of the film, were employed to establish narrative, genre and tone, and Porter's use of this violent image that literally assaulted the audience is a clear indicator of the significance of violence to the earliest cinematic pioneers. Importantly, this kind of violence was not just an American preoccupation; films like *The Great Train Robbery* and the Biograph Company's comic film *The Escaped Lunatic* (1903) were influenced specifically by a series of imported British films about violent criminals being pursued by the authorities (see Musser 1990: 352).

As the cinema continued to develop and mature, filmmakers followed their instincts in continuing to work violence into both the storylines and the visual spectacle. Few at this time were better than D. W. Griffith, whose controversial epic *The Birth of a Nation* (1915) featured large-scale battle sequences and a scene in which a young woman avoids being raped by jumping off a cliff to her death, which in typical silent-era style is not immediate, but comes after prolonged and theatrical death throes in the arms of her beloved. The racially charged violence of these scenes was answered by the black novelist-turned-independent film pioneer Oscar Micheaux, who in 1919 wrote, produced and directed *Within Our Gates*, a daring look at racial violence that reversed the rape threat from *The Birth of a Nation* by depicting a white man attempting to rape a black woman. The violence is 'depicted with a luridness and savagery rare in the American cinema' of the era (McGilligan 2007: 143), particularly in the film's most notorious and then-unheard-of scene, which depicts an entire black family being lynched, which Gerard R. Butters Jr describes in the following manner: 'This series of shots remain the most remarkable in African-American silent film. They are well edited and graphic, heightening the tension and frustration of the audience' (2000: Part 2, para. 11).

Meanwhile, Griffith continued to churn out films: more than four hundred one-reelers for the Biograph Company, many of which were exceedingly popular re-enactments of Civil War battles and Indian raids. While the violence in these films is frequent, it is not particularly graphic, which cannot be said about Griffith's next feature-length film, *Intolerance* (1916). During the Babylonian battle sequence, the film shows two bloody onscreen decapitations, bodies being pierced by arrows and the most viscerally striking shot of all: a soldier driving a spear into the naked stomach

An onscreen decapitation provides surprisingly graphic violence: *Intolerance* (1916)

of another soldier, causing blood to gush out. Although, as noted, explicit violence of this sort was not particularly frequent in silent-era cinema, Griffith was not alone in his experimentations with depicting the damage physical violence does to the human body. Although the silent films of Cecil B. DeMille are often discussed in relation to their incorporation of overt sexuality into narratives of strict Victorian morality, many of his films also include moments of still-shocking violence, including a scene in *The Cheat* (1915) in which Hishuru Tori (Sessue Hayakawa) brands the shoulder of Edith Hardy (Fannie Ward), leaving a large wound that she will later bare in a court of law to justify her shooting him in retaliation.[1] Relatively graphic scenes of violence are also present in early sound films such as Lewis Milestone's 1930 version of *All Quiet on the Western Front*, which depicts a soldier being hit by a grenade while charging the German trenches, leaving only his dismembered hands hanging onto the coils of a barbed wire fence.

Outside of the United States other filmmakers were also devising ways to increase the impact of violence onscreen, sometimes for simple shock value and other times for explicitly ideological purposes. Overwhelmed by the devastation of World War One and the national disillusionment that followed, the nascent German film industry produced expressionistic films whose 'overtones of death, horror, and nightmare' seemed to 'the tortured souls of contemporary Germany' to be 'the reflection of its own grimacing image, offering a kind of release' (Eisner 1973: 17). *Das Cabinet des Dr. Caligari* (*The Cabinet of Dr. Caligari*, 1919) presented an apparent madman with hypnotic powers who could lead another person to kill indiscriminately; in *Nosferatu* (1922), F. W. Murnau gave us the first screen vampire, an unromanticised monstrosity with a seething appetite for blood; and in *Dr. Mabuse, der Spieler – Ein Bild der Zeit* (*Dr. Mabuse, the Gambler*, 1922), Fritz Lang presented a vision of terroristic criminality that reverberates all too well today. Meanwhile, in the groundbreaking Danish documentary/horror film *Häxan* (*The Witch*, 1922), Benjamin Christensen, one of the most inventive and daring of silent film directors, depicted a litany of unsettling images, including a witch pulling a severed human hand out of a bundle of sticks and snapping off a finger for a potion, and a demon bleeding an infant corpse over a cauldron. Such scenes were enough to cause a critic for the trade journal *Variety* to write, 'Wonderful though this picture is, it is absolutely unfit for public exhibition' (Anon. 1923: 30). Elsewhere, Luis Buñuel and Salvador Dalí were experimenting with surrealist images in their notorious short film *Un chien andalou*, whose most infamous scene depicts a man (Buñuel himself) slicing a woman's eyeball with a straight razor in extreme close-up. The scene is carefully constructed to fulfil the surrealist imperative to shock and outrage, a literal and figurative attack on vision, and to judge its lasting effectiveness one only has to view the film in a roomful of jaded undergraduate students and hear the collective gasp that accompanies this moment. The film also features nightmarish images of ants crawling out of a wound in a man's palm and a woman poking at a dismembered hand with a stick.

One of the most important examples of sustained violence in the silent era is the Odessa Steps sequence in Sergei Eisenstein's *Bronenosets Potyomkin* (*Battleship Potemkin*, 1926). The lengthy sequence depicts Czarist soldiers gunning down unarmed civilians who are supportive of a mutinous ship during the failed 1909 uprising in Russia. The severe nature of Eisenstein's montage editing inherently emphasises the violence of the scene, which makes sense given the filmmaker's theoretical contention that 'art is always conflict' (1957: 46). Although he sometimes presents the violence in an abstract way that averts our gaze from physical damage (for example, a close-up of a man's knees buckling followed by a first-person view as he begins to tumble down the steps), Eisenstein also presents the violence of the massacre in unequivocal terms: blood streams down a screaming child's face after he is shot in the back, a woman's white gloves are stained as she clutches at her bleeding stomach, and, in the sequence's gruesome visual climax, there is a stunning shock cut to a woman with her right eye shot out, blood running from beneath her shattered glasses. From a narrative perspective, the violence is further heightened by the fact that there is no discerning among victims, whether they be women, children or the elderly. It is, without doubt, a savage and deeply disturbing portrait of human violence and one of the finest examples of the emotional and political impact film violence can have.

Censorship of violent images in Hollywood cinema

While the majority of early regulation aimed at motion picture content is commonly associated with the control of sexual images, there were also grave concerns about the violent nature of the cinema and the dangerous social effects associated with it. In fact, in the first US court case involving the censorship of motion pictures, *Block v. the City of Chicago* (1909), a group of six nickelodeon owners led by Jake Block challenged the City of Chicago's 1907 movie censorship ordinance (the first in the country) after two films, *The James Boys of Missouri* and *Night Riders* (both 1908), were denied licences due to their violent content. Also, when the first federal censorship bill, the Smith-Hughes Picture Censorship Bill, was proposed in 1914, it was oddly specific regarding certain kinds of inappropriate violence, while maintaining a more general tone in other matters. It proposed the creation of a Federal Motion Picture Commission as part of the Bureau of Education, and the purpose of the Commission would be 'to censor all films, endorsing the good and condemning those which come under the specifications of what is "obscene, indecent, immoral, inhuman, or those that depict a bull-fight, or a prizefight, or that will corrupt or impair the morals of children or incite to crime"' (Harriet S. Pritchard, 'A Federal Motion Picture Commission', *Signal*, May 21, 1914: 10, cited in Parker 1996: 81).

As Stephen Prince (2003) has argued, control over violent content in the silent and classical eras of Hollywood cinema had less to do with the specifics of how the violence was presented than the violent actions themselves. This is why the term *violence* was rarely used in public and political discourse about the cinema until the late 1950s and early 1960s, when it became 'a concept with explanatory force' (Barker 2004: 58). Prior to that time, the real issue on people's minds was *crime*, particularly violent crime like robbery and murder, both of which were popular topics in the cinema from its inception. Reform groups were certainly concerned about violence being graphically presented onscreen, but their primary concern was the depiction of criminality and how it might appeal to and therefore possibly influence the morals of the audience. Thus, early attempts to control the violent content of Hollywood films were first and foremost defined by a concern as to how depictions of criminality might unduly influence viewers. Accusations in the national press of real-life crimes being inspired, if not literally caused, by movies were common. Fear of 'copycat crime' was rampant, particularly because it offered an easy and identifiable scapegoat for complex issues that had deep and uncomfortable social roots. So, for example, in 1912 the *Philadelphia Record* tried to pin a boy's attempt to rob a train on *The Great Train Robbery* even though there was no proof he had ever seen the film and at least part of his plan (waiting for the train whistle to blow to cover the sound of his gunshot) could not have been learned from the film (see Brownlow 1990: 168).

If a film had to contain some violent material for narrative purposes – and many did – then a secondary concern was how that violence was presented. For reform groups and socially conscious politicians, the prevailing view was that film violence should be as discreet and tasteful as possible. In 1909, the People's Institute, a progressive reform group, created the National Board of Censorship (renamed the National Board of Review in 1916) at the behest of New York exhibitors who were eager to avoid Mayor George B. McClellan closing down all the city's movie houses, as he had done in December 1908. In order to prove that they could police themselves and thus escape the omnipresent shadowy threat of federal censorship, the studios willingly submitted their films for review and paid a fee to the Board, which then certified the films that conformed to contemporary social and moral norms. The Board adopted eight prohibitive standards to guide their certification process, two of which dealt directly with violence. The first prohibition, 'undue depictions of crime', dealt with the *what*, while the second prohibition, 'unnecessary elaboration or prolongation of suffering, brutality, vulgarity, violence, or crime', dealt with the *how*.

When the US film industry came together in the early 1920s and formed its own trade organisation, the Motion Picture Producers and Distributors of America (MPPDA) under the leadership of former Postmaster General Will Hays, one of its first missions was to create a formal document outlining the kinds of material that were and were not appropriate for respectable motion pictures. This began in 1924 when the MPPDA produced 'The Formula', which Kevin S. Sandler describes as 'a vague list of instructions for scrutinising source material such as books or plays for screen presentation' (2007: 20). Three years later 'The Formula' was replaced with 'The Don'ts and Be Carefuls', a more specific list of things that should either never be depicted in Hollywood films or should be treated with great care. Any reference to film violence is notably absent from the 'don'ts', which reflects the industry's realisation of the vast popularity of violence, although there are quite a few of the 'be carefuls' that relate to violent behaviours and their depictions. In fact, of the 25 listed 'be carefuls', ten are somehow related to film violence:

3. Arson
4. The use of firearms
5. Theft, robbery, safecracking, and dynamiting of trains, mines, buildings, etc. (having in mind the effect which a too-detailed description of these may have upon the moron)
6. Brutality and possible gruesomeness
7. Technique of committing murder by whatever method
10. Actual hangings or electrocutions as legal punishment for crime
14. Apparent cruelty to children and animals
15. Branding of people or animals
17. Rape or attempted rape
22. Surgical operations (quoted in Miller 1994: 40)

This demonstrates that, despite allowing such imagery, the MPPDA was exceedingly wary of the potential consequences for the industry in terms of arousing controversy and government intervention.

In 1930, the MPPDA expanded on the 'Don'ts and Be Carefuls' and created the Production Code, a formal document that contained explicit instructions on how to handle film content narratively and visually, although it was not fully enforced until 1934 with the creation of the Production Code Administration (PCA). While the Code is most frequently discussed in terms of how it addressed sexual morality, issues of film violence are actually the first subject considered in the Code's 'Particular Applications' (which was amended to the Code in 1934) under the heading 'Crimes Against the Law'. This section addressed not only the moral issue of never 'throw[ing] sympathy with the crime', but also specifically forbade presenting brutal killings in detail and restricted the use of firearms to 'the essentials'. This ensured that the stylistic approaches filmmakers used to depict violence had to be significantly reduced, meaning that violence in Hollywood films of the classical era would be largely unrealistic and pain-free. The last section of the 'Particular Applications', labelled 'Repellent Subjects', warned filmmakers of the following:

The following subjects must be treated within the careful limits of good taste:

1. *Actual hangings* or electrocutions as legal punishments for crime
2. *Third Degree* methods
3. *Brutality* and possible gruesomeness
4. *Branding* of people or animals
5. *Apparent cruelty* to children or animals
6. *The sale of women*, or a woman selling her virtue
7. *Surgical operations* (quoted in Leff and Simmons 1990: 286; emphasis in original)[2]

However, even with these specific admonishments, some bits of graphic violence still showed up in studio-produced films. For example, in 20th Century-Fox's *Show Them No Mercy* (1935), veteran director George Marshall depicted bullet wounds on a victim by firing inked plugs at a clear screen in front of the actor (see Prince 2003: 119).

Thus, even though the enforcement of the Production Code's strictures largely eliminated the graphic display of onscreen violence from the 1930s until the final dismantling of the Code in the late 1960s, violence persisted because the Code never decreed that violent subjects had to be avoided altogether, as it did with some other subjects (such as 'sex perversion', 'white slavery' and 'pointed profanity'). Strangulation (as in *Double Indemnity*, 1944), dismemberment (for example, in *Rear Window*, 1954), torture (as in *Kiss Me Deadly*, 1955) and bodily mutilation (for example, in *The Searchers*, 1956) were all acceptable parts of a film narrative as long as they were depicted using a complex series of aesthetic strategies described by Stephen Prince as 'substitutional poetics' (2003: 205). These included tactics such as spatial displacement (placing the violence offscreen), metonymic displacement (allowing something onscreen to 'stand in' for the violence), substitutional emblematics (displacing the physical wounding of the body onto other objects) and emotional bracketing (a brief respite in which viewers can 'recover' after a violent episode). These tactics, which formed the dominant means by which violence was conveyed prior to the 1960s, created what Prince calls an 'unstable equilibrium' (2003: 206) of classical film violence: owing to changes in style and various periods in which enforcement of the Code was either relaxed or strengthened, films of this era contained both direct and indirect violence. In this way, unlike other production processes and aspects of film style that developed in response to economic issues and narrative requirements, the depiction of violence in the classical Hollywood era was shaped almost entirely by the filmmakers having to adhere to the tenets of the Code.

Violence during the classical era (1920s–1950s)

The appeal of real-life criminality and violence as subjects for fictional films dates back to the beginnings of cinema, as we have seen with the popularity of early recreations of executions and war atrocities. Throughout the 1910s and 1920s the Hollywood studios produced numerous films whose stories of murder were ripped straight from the day's headlines, some of which even starred the actual people whose lives were being depicted (see Miller 1994: 23). Organised crime, with its inherent intrigue and drama, provided an obvious source for early movies, and it should come as little surprise that D. W. Griffith was among the first to exploit the subject. His 1912 film *The Musketeers of Pig Alley*, which was inspired by newspaper accounts of the shooting of a New York gambler named Herman Rosenthal, is generally considered the first gangster film, and studios continued to produce such films throughout the 1920s, including *Lights of New York* (1928), the first all-talking synchronised sound feature.

While most of these movies had a moralising tone that viewed the gangsters from a social-reform perspective, beginning with *The Racket* (1927) and *Underworld* (1928) they began to shift their perspective to that of the gangster himself, which fundamentally altered the genre and its violence (see Munby 1999: 25). The gangster film ushered in new levels of screen violence, especially with the addition of sound in the late 1920s, which allowed audiences to hear the shrieking tyres of speeding cars and, most importantly, the explosive firepower of Tommy guns. The infamous triumvirate of early 1930s gangster films – *Little Caesar* (1930), *The Public Enemy* (1931) and *Scarface* (1932) – challenged public conceptions of how criminal violence could be deployed in studio films.[3] Onscreen violence increased substantially in these films, to the point that Stephen Prince argues that *Scarface* 'exhibits the kind of sustained, hypnotised fascination with violence that has become an everyday feature of contemporary film. That is, quite simply, ultraviolence of a very modern kind' (2003: 113). Such imagery caused shock and outrage on numerous fronts; writing on the front page of *Film Daily*, Jack Alicoate wrote that *Scarface* caused 'a distinct feeling of nausea' and the film's subject matter 'simply do[es] not belong on the screen' (quoted in Doherty 1999: 149), and Will Hays eventually declared a moratorium on the genre in July 1935 (see Munby 1999). Although cut short by the industry that created them, the gangster cycle still had a lasting impact on the cinema. Richard Maltby (2001) writes that the problem was not so much the specific violence of the films, but rather the performative appeal of the gangster (anti)heroes and their criminality. At the time of *Scarface*'s release, producer Howard Hughes grumbled that the film was targeted by corrupt politicians who resented its 'unpleasant political truths' (see Doherty 1999: 150), which again suggests that controlling violent imagery is frequently used as a means of displacing other concerns. Not surprisingly, the 'problem' of gangster films was solved not by removing such violence from the screen, but by relocating it to the other side of the law, so that James Cagney, who had become a star with his career-defining role as the gangster Tom Powers in *The Public Enemy*, could be an enforcer of the law in *G Men* (1935).[4]

In addition to the gangster film, violence in American cinema was deeply affected by Universal Studios' cycle of Gothic horror movies, including *Dracula* (1931), *Frankenstein* (1931), *The Mummy* (1932) and *Bride of Frankenstein* (1935). Referred to in the trade papers as 'nightmare pictures', these films caused their spectators genuine consternation, sometimes leading to audience walk-outs, as was the case when Universal previewed *Frankenstein* (see Doherty 1999: 300). PTA executive Marjorie Ross Davis walked out after the first 15 minutes of *Dracula*, claiming that she 'could stand no more' and demanding that it 'be withdrawn from public viewing' because of the threat to children posed by its 'insane horrible details' (quoted in Schechter 2005: 118). Nightmare pictures, such as these from 1932, dabbled in all kinds of perverse violence, including cannibalistic murder (*Doctor X*), extended images of torture (*Murders in the Rue Morgue*) and the presentation of monstrosities and misshapen humans, both fictional (*The Island of Lost Souls*) and real (*Freaks*). These films helped introduce a kind of sadistic violence that had not been seen in movies before, and although the violence of both the horror and gangster films was not explicitly forbidden by the Production Code, both genres constantly ran afoul of local and state censors and were eventually banned outright, the former in Great Britain and the latter in the United States.

During World War Two, American filmmakers were able to increase the graphic representations of violence in war films, partially because viewers were being regularly exposed to newsreels and documentaries – 'vivid anthologies of atrocities committed by the Germans and Japanese' (Leach 1975: 73). Although war films still utilised unrealistic visual codes such as the 'clutch and fall' manner of gracefully dying after being shot, many of them pushed aggressively at the limitations of film violence. In *Bataan* (1943), a soldier is nearly decapitated onscreen, and in *Pride of the Marines* (1945) an exploding squib shows the immediate physical impact of a bullet in a soldier's arm. In that same film a US Marine is shot in the head (a rarity in and of itself for studio cinema at the time), which is clearly depicted both visually (his helmet bends inward and a puff of smoke bursts out of the hole) and aurally (on the soundtrack we hear the thud of the bullet). This realism is compromised by the character's actual death, which is depicted by a graceful and unrealistic sinking to the ground, but then reasserted with a close-up of his dead face – 'unmistakably a body done to death by violence, without the cosmetic gloss that typically surrounded violent death in [classic Hollywood] movies' (Prince 2003: 157). This kind of uneven treatment of onscreen violence had been seen before, for example in a scene near the end of *Hell's Angels* (1930) in which Ben Lyon (Monte Rutledge) is shot in the back. The wound is visualised onscreen by actually shooting Rutledge in the back with an ink-soaked plug of sponge rubber from a starting pistol, thus creating the illusion of a bloody wound suddenly appearing (see Cook 1999: 131). However, the relative realism of this wounding is immediately undermined by the melodramatic and drawn-out death scene that follows.

Not surprisingly, the increasingly graphic nature of film violence in World War Two films did not dissipate during the postwar era. As James Naremore notes, 'It was violence, not sex, that accounted for the most visible changes in the standards of motion-picture censorship during the 1940s and early 1950s' (1998: 102). Censors in other countries took note of the rising tide of American film violence, evidenced by the British Board of Film Censors complaining to the Hollywood industry in 1948 and 1949 about the amount of violence in their films. Gordon Mirams, the chief government censor and film registrar in New Zealand, took it upon himself to make an 'objective analysis' of one hundred feature films (seventy from the US and thirty non-US) distributed in New Zealand during a five-month period (December 1949 to April 1950), after which he concluded that only one-sixth of the English-language films he examined were completely free of crime and violence (see Mirams 1951).[5] Writing in the pages of *Hollywood Quarterly* in 1947, John Houseman noted the prevalence of prison, prize-fighting and crime films, which he described as having 'sprung from the common ground of violence which is still a characteristic of our times and of our tastes in entertainment' (1947: 65).

In particular, postwar crime films (many of which are now categorised as film noir) reflected the changes in how violence was depicted onscreen both visually and thematically. In *Brute Force* (1947), which Houseman criticised for its 'contrived' brutalities and 'story-conference' sadism (1947: 63), a guard beats a prisoner with a length of rubber hose, a stool pigeon is threatened with a blowtorch to the face until he falls back into a press that crushes him, and a climactic attempted prison break results in the machine-gunning of dozens of people. Gendered violence was particularly prevalent in film noir; for example, in *Kiss of Death* (1947), a deranged gangster pushes a disabled woman in a wheelchair down a flight of stairs to her death, in both *Raw Deal* (1948) and *The Big Heat* (1953) women are viciously scalded by sadistic male characters (with flaming fondue in the former and hot coffee in the latter), and *Kiss Me Deadly* begins with a woman being tortured to death with a pair of pliers (offscreen, of course, but with anguished screams telling us all we need to know) and ends with the *femme fatale* being incinerated alive by an exploding atomic device. At the same time, though, women could be just as violent as men, as evidenced in *Gun Crazy* (1949), which predates *Bonnie and Clyde* with its romanticised story of an outlaw couple on the run. The film, which was originally released with the unambiguous title *Deadly is the Female*, concerns Bart Tare (John Dall), a young man who is goaded by his wife Annie Laurie Starr (Peggy Cummins) into joining her on a cross-country spree of armed robberies. While Bart is obsessed with guns, he refuses to use them to kill. Annie, on the other hand, has no such restraint, and at the end of the film Bart is forced to kill her to keep her from shooting his childhood friends, who are now police officers. While Bart's moral qualms about violence were largely the result of changes required by the Production Code to introduce a moral voice to the film's lurid narrative (see Prince 2003: 134–6), the ultimate result is a portrait of psychotic female violence that can be contained only by death.

The violence of these crime films was also a defining characteristic of juvenile delinquent (JD) films, which became increasingly popular in the 1950s. Such films had been around for decades, with peaks of popularity in the 'Jazz Age' and the 1930s Dead End Kids films (see Doherty 1988). However, there was something fundamentally different about the JD films of the 1950s, partially because they tapped so directly into widespread social fears that culminated in the publication of three reports by a Senate Judiciary Subcommittee that tied juvenile delinquency to movies, comic books and television. Films like *The Wild One* (1953), *Blackboard Jungle* (1955), *Rebel Without a Cause* (1955) and *Teenage Crime Wave* (1955) depicted purposefully 'shocking' youthful violence that was often aimed directly at adult society and was all the more unnerving because the perpetrators were often middle class, thus denying an easy socio-economic explanation for their problems. However, as with the gangster film of the 1930s, most of these movies were tempered with a social didacticism that made them fundamentally divided. As Thomas Doherty puts it, 'virtually all delinquent films revel in their portrayal of juvenile violence at the same time they preach the ultimate squelching of the perpetrators' (1988: 134).

These more intense forms of postwar film violence also found their way into the western genre, which was recast in the 1950s with morally con-flicted and deeply violent characters. One of the most powerful examples is John Ford's *The Searchers*, which cast John Wayne as Ethan Edwards, a lonely, bitter and racist antihero in a film that is simultaneously a rous-ing adventure story, a fable about the nature of quest and fulfilment, and an exploration of the racism that created such intense violence between Native Americans and encroaching white settlers. While all the most grue-some violence takes place offscreen, it is still hard not to wince when Ethan shoots out the eyes of a dead Comanche warrior or refuses to discuss his traumatic discovery of a horribly mutilated body (for more about *The Searchers*, see chapter three). From a purely visual standpoint, however, it was George Stevens' *Shane* (1953) that helped intensify the physical depictions of violence in the western. The bar brawl between Shane (Alan Ladd) and Chris Calloway (Ben Johnson) is a notably sweaty, gritty and bloody affair, but it is the scene in which Jack Wilson (Jack Palance) shoots and kills Frank 'Stonewall' Torrey (Elisha Cook Jr) that made a real impact. Rather than sinking and dying gracefully, Stonewall's body is blown sev-eral feet backwards by the force of the bullet, which gives this moment of violence a decidedly modern feel. More will be said about the western genre and its use of violence in chapter three.

Escalating violence in 1950s European and Asian cinema

In the late 1950s, Hammer Films, a minor British studio, began producing updated versions of the same Gothic stories that had fuelled the 1930s Universal horror films, except with more sexual suggestiveness and dis-plays of bloodletting that were, most importantly, in Technicolor. Images of violence on film now had vibrant hues, rather than shades of grey. Beginning with *The Curse of Frankenstein* (1957) and *Dracula* (aka *Horror of Dracula*, 1958), these films were hugely successful in both the UK and the US[6] and helped raise the threshold of what kinds of images were not only permissible, but expected in horror films. Although rather tame by today's standards, the jars of eyeballs and dismembered hands in *The Curse of Frankenstein* and the scene in *Dracula* in which a stake is driven into a vam-pire's heart and blood spurts out were genuinely shocking to audiences in the 1950s and early 1960s. Interestingly, there were different versions of many Hammer films depending on the country in which they were showing.

According to Carlos Clarens, for the early Hammer films there were usually three different versions prepared: 'one for the United States, a milder one for Great Britain, and one considerably stronger for Japan' (1967: 143).[7]

However, Hammer was not alone in raising the gore threshold in British filmmaking. Cinematographer-turned-director Arthur Crabtree's *Horrors of the Black Museum* (1959) opens with a scene in which a woman is killed by a pair of binoculars that impale her eyeballs with retractable knives. Although the actual impaling takes place offscreen, Crabtree shows us a medium close-up of the victim screaming and holding her hands to her eyes with bright red blood running through her fingers, and then cuts to a shot of puddles of blood on the floor. That same year Robert Day directed *Corridors of Blood*, which paired horror icons Boris Karloff and Christopher Lee and mixed horror tropes with a fictionalised historical drama about the discovery of anaesthesia. The film contains several boundary-pushing scenes: one in which Dr Bolton (Karloff) slices across a moaning patient's leg during an amputation, a close-up of Resurrection Joe (Lee) stabbing a knife into the back of a night watchman and then pulling it out, and another close-up of Joe stabbing Dr Bolton in the gut, followed by Bolton flinging a beaker of acid into Joe's face. All of these shots had to be removed at the behest of the Production Code Administration before the film could be approved for theatrical distribution in the United States.[8]

At the same time, something similar was happening in Italian cinema. In the Gothic romance *La frusta e il corpo* (*The Whip and the Body*, 1963), director Mario Bava pays scrupulous attention to the horrid physicality of various whippings, moving the camera in lovingly whenever the heroine's bare back is being lashed. The physicality in and of itself was quite shocking, but even more so was the heroine's eroticised reaction to the brutality. The mixing of sex and violence is always an uneasy concoction, and Bava's film makes the connection clearly and unequivocally. Italian filmmakers were also increasing the levels of violence in that most American of genres, the western. Of predominant importance are Sergio Leone's spaghetti western trilogy, *Per un pugno di dollari* (*A Fistful of Dollars*, 1964), *Per qualche dollaro in più* (*For a Few Dollars More*, 1965) and *Il buono, il brutto, il cattivo* (*The Good, the Bad, and the Ugly*, 1966), all of which were popular in American movie houses. According to Jake Horsley, it was the 'wantonness' of the violence, not its 'intensity', that 'caused such a stir among audiences and filmmakers' (1999a: 25). Similarly, Stephen Prince argues that, while there was little spurting blood in Leone's films, they helped 'shear screen violence free of the reassuring moral context that had always governed it in past films' (1998: 18). While there were numerous directors associated with spaghetti westerns, they all shared in common 'a uniformly grotesque vision' in which the western 'becomes a potential inferno, a journey into hell and, possibly, back' (Kaminsky 1976: 47–8). Yet, the tone of the violence in spaghetti westerns could sometimes be wildly inconsistent. In Sergio Corbucci's *Django* (1966), for example, some of the violence borders on the comical, such as when Django (Franco Nero), who has been dragging a coffin behind him since the opening scene, finally reveals what he has been carrying in it when he unexpectedly pulls out a Gatling gun and proceeds to mow down an army of opponents. At the same time, the film features other scenes that are quite stomach-churning, including one in which Django's hands are beaten to a bloody pulp with the butt of a rifle. An already heightened genre to begin with, spaghetti westerns continued to escalate into near absurdity throughout the late 1960s and early 1970s, with filmmakers trying to up the ante on bloodshed, sadism and nihilism, culminating in films such as Lucio Fulci's *I quattro dell'apocalisse* (*Four for the Apocalypse*, 1975), which includes scenes of a man being skinned alive, cannibalism and the shotgun massacre of an entire town.

Meanwhile, Japanese filmmakers, who had been restricted throughout the late 1940s and early 1950s by the occupying Allied armies who disallowed samurai films (*chanbara*) because they tended to glorify nationalism and feudalism, returned with a vengeance by experimenting with more explicit and aesthetically complicated forms of violence. This was particularly true of the new spate of samurai films, which as a genre centre on characters whose fundamental trait is an almost supernatural ability to kill, sometimes dozens of opponents at a time. Akira Kurosawa was one of the primary innovators in using slow-motion to enhance the effect of violent action, particularly in depicting death, a practice that would be picked up by Arthur Penn in *The Left Handed Gun* (1958) and then greatly expanded by Penn in *Bonnie and Clyde* and Sam Peckinpah in *The Wild Bunch*. Stephen Prince cites a scene in *Shichinin no samurai* (*Seven Samurai*, 1954) in which the samurai leader Kambei (Takashi Shimura) kills a thief, whose death is depicted in a series of shots that intercut regular and slow-motion, as a crucial development in the history of aestheticising violence (1998: 54). Kurosawa also made action violence more bloody in

This legendary arterial spray elevates levels of violence: *Sanjuro* (1962)

Yojimbo (1961) and *Tsubaki Sanjûrô* (*Sanjuro*, 1962), both of which draw heavily on the iconography of the American western. *Yojimbo* opens with the protagonist, a nameless samurai played by Toshiro Mifune, wandering into a seemingly quiet village and being met not by a person, but by a dog happily trotting down the town's main street with a dismembered human hand in his mouth – a humorously gruesome, nearly surreal, image that immediately sets the tone for things to come. Blood spatters when people are cut down in the film's numerous fight scenes, and at one point we see a full shot of a man's arm being cut off, although the gruesomeness of these images is alleviated slightly by their being in black-and-white. In the final showdown in *Sanjuro*, the titular protagonist (again played by Mifune) faces off with his chief rival, Hanbei Muroto (Tatsuya Nakadai, who also played his nemesis in *Yojimbo*), and dispatches him with one sword stroke, resulting in a legendary, over-the-top arterial spray – a literal geyser of blood – which had never been seen in a film of this type.

Such exaggerated blood spray was soon to become a staple of samurai and kung fu movies, particularly in the 1970s. Kung fu movies turned violence into performative display akin to musical numbers, which troubled many viewers who were not comfortable with violence being made graceful (see Kaminsky 1976). In sometimes stark contrast to the grace and beauty of bodies in motion, kung fu films also paid special attention to the images of bloodied bodies and the hyper-realised sounds of cracking bones and tearing flesh. The genre reached a culmination of sorts with *Gekitotsu! Satsujin ken* (*The Street Fighter*, 1974), in which Takuma Tsurugi (Sonny

Chiba) literally rips pieces of his opponents' bodies off with his bare hands (in one scene he tears off a would-be rapist's genitals and in another scene he digs into an opponent's throat and tears out his Adam's apple). The film was notorious in the United States for being the first to be rated X for violence by the Classification and Rating Administration (CARA) of the Motion Picture Association of America, which some New York City theatres proudly advertised on their marquees (see Jonas 1975). Also of note are the films produced in Hong Kong at the Shaw Studios in the 1960s and 1970s, including those of the prolific director Chang Cheh, who mentored future director John Woo and helped refine the highly operatic style of slow-motion violence in films such as *Bian cheng san xia* (*The Magnificent Trio*, 1966) and *Ci Ma* (*Blood Brothers*, 1973).

Film violence in the 1960s: from the grindhouse to the mainstream

It was during the 1960s that film violence underwent its most radical and rapid developments in both the United States and Europe, with graphic displays of violence steadily migrating from the margins into the mainstream and forever altering what was possible both visually and ideologically in popular cinema. The decade opened with a triumvirate of violent and disturbing films made by highly respected filmmakers in different countries – Michael Powell's *Peeping Tom* (1960) in England, Alfred Hitchcock's *Psycho* (1960) in the US and Georges Franju's *Les yeux sans visage* (*Eyes Without a Face*, 1960) in France – each of which was disparaged by its country's critical establishment and only belatedly recognised as a cinematic landmark. As Joan Hawkins (2000) notes, all three of these films occupy contested cultural space in which they are simultaneously revered cinematic masterpieces and the forebears of that most culturally despised of genres, the splatter film.[9]

Michael Powell's *Peeping Tom* is a powerful psychological thriller about a soft-spoken serial killer who uses a retractable blade in his camera tripod to kill young women and immortalise their terror on film. While the vast majority of the violence is kept just offscreen, the idea in the film is highly unnerving in the way it captures the metaphorical essence of the horror genre (see Clover 1992). It was so unnerving, in fact, that Powell's career was virtually destroyed by the vitriol heaped on the film by British critics (see Christie 1978).

Later that same year, Alfred Hitchcock shocked American audiences with *Psycho*, a film of such standing in the annals of film history that many have forgotten how many critics initially dismissed it as a sick, twisted waste of the director's time and talent. Even those critics who wrote positively about the film as a whole still registered disgust with its depiction of violence. The most telling response came from Stanley Kauffman, who called the two murders in *Psycho* 'among the most vicious I have ever seen in films, with Hitchcock employing his considerable skill … to shock us past horror-entertainment into resentment' (1960: 22). Audiences were certainly shocked, as the unexpected murder of the protagonist Marion Crane (Janet Leigh) in the shower some 45 minutes into the film resulted in 'gasps, screams, yells, even running up and down the aisles', all of which was 'unprecedented' (Williams 1994: 15). However, this shock did not translate into resentment, but rather a desire for more, which helps explain why the British and American film markets were flooded in subsequent years with so many *Psycho*-inspired films and outright knock-offs (*Homicidal*, 1961; *Maniac*, 1962; *Paranoiac*, 1962; *Whatever Happened to Baby Jane?*, 1962; *Nightmare*, 1963; *Strait-Jacket*, 1964), most of which increased the violence, but none of which, with the exception of Roman Polanski's *Repulsion* (1965), equalled Hitchcock's mastery of technique.

The same year that Hitchcock was shocking American audiences, Georges Franju, co-founder of France's esteemed Cinémathèque Française, scandalised his country with his second feature film, *Eyes Without a Face*, which, along with Henri-George Clouzot's *Les diaboliques* (1954), was a rare French entry into the horror genre. The story of a plastic surgeon who murders young women in a failing effort to restore the brutally disfigured face of his beloved daughter, *Eyes Without a Face* is a visually elegant, but disturbing portrait of a scientist playing God for intensely personal reasons. Like *Psycho*, the film's notoriety centred primarily around one particular scene in which Franju depicts with coldly calculated long takes the surgeon removing a woman's face. Initial audiences were floored – some literally when they fainted – as Franju's camera did not flinch when the scalpel began drawing a bloody line through the flesh, culminating in the uncanny image of the entire face being lifted off.

While films like *Peeping Tom*, *Psycho* and *Eyes Without a Face* were challenging the boundaries of violence in mainstream theatres, films playing on the rural drive-in and urban grindhouse circuit were shattering them.

The European horror and Asian kung fu movies discussed in the previous section made the rounds on this circuit in badly dubbed versions, as did the emergent exploitation films known as 'ghoulies' and 'roughies', which took the voyeuristic logic of nudie films to increasingly sadistic extremes.[10] As Eddie Muller and Daniel Faris put it, 'lust led to violence' (1996: 95) in films such as *Scum of the Earth* (1963), *The Defilers* (1965), *The Animal* (1968) and *Hot Spur* (1969), all of which featured levels of sexual violence that were rarely if ever seen in the mainstream cinema. At the same time, serious-minded European filmmakers were dealing thoughtfully with sexualised violence in films like Vittorio De Sica's *La ciociara* (*Two Women,* 1960), in which a mother and her 13-year-old daughter are gang-raped by Moroccan soldiers while escaping the bombings in World War Two, and Ingmar Bergman's allegorical *Jungfrukällan* (*The Virgin Spring*, 1960), whose rape scene had to be trimmed before the Production Code Administration would allow it to play in US theatres.

More graphic forms of visual violence were also being forged by low-budget genre filmmakers, both in the United States and abroad. In *A Bucket of Blood* (1959), Roger Corman featured a victim whose head has been split open and another who has been decapitated. However, the onscreen representations of this gore are ameliorated by the fact that the murderer, a sad-sack would-be artist played by Dick Miller, encases the corpses in clay and passes them off as sculptures; thus, even though the split skull has gory detail, it is not actually representing flesh and bone. No such distance is offered in Nobuo Nakagawa's *Jigoku* (1960), a horror film whose explicit depiction of the torments of the Eight Hells is in direct contrast to the more moody and elegant approach used in contemporaneous Japanese horror films like Masaki Kobayashi's *Kwaidan* (1964). Although obviously working on a limited budget (the film was made for the struggling Shintoho Studios, an exploitation outfit that would go bankrupt the following year), Nakagawa stages an impressive series of disturbing visual images: lakes of blood, rivers of pus, boiling cauldrons and fields of metal spikes, as well as hands cut off, eyes gouged out, teeth smashed in and one poor victim reduced to a flayed skeleton who can only stare horrified at his own beating heart.

While *Jigoku* and other Japanese horror films had limited or no distribution in the West at this time, the flag of visceral onscreen gore was being taken up in the United States by Herschell Gordon Lewis and his pioneering 'gore films'. Lewis was a former college literature professor-turned-director of nudie films who ventured into graphic violence because onscreen nudity was becoming too common and he was looking for something new to exploit. In *Blood Feast* (1963), *Two Thousand Maniacs* (1964) and *Color Me Blood Red* (1965), Lewis and his producing partner David F. Friedman far surpassed what had been seen on the screen before, constructing their films around threadbare plots in which people were dismembered, gutted, beheaded, crushed or otherwise killed in some imaginatively grisly manner, albeit with often unconvincing special effects.[11] A few years later, George A. Romero took Lewis's use of visceral onscreen gore and connected it to American cultural and familial discontent in *Night of the Living Dead* (1968), a low-budget, independently produced black-and-white horror film about survivors trapped in a farmhouse during a zombie plague. Romero's vivid depiction of zombies gnawing the flesh off charred human remains and a child zombie hacking her mother to death and then feeding on the corpse were not just visually shocking, but thematically shocking with their undeniable social, political, moral and racial undercurrents. While *Night of the Living Dead* was not highly regarded on its initial release,[12] it quickly gained critical acceptance and within a year was being invited to play as part of the Museum of Modern Art's Cineprobe series (see Hoberman & Rosenbaum 1983: 113).

Night of the Living Dead's simultaneous acceptance on the grindhouse/drive-in circuit and in the hallowed halls of intellectual cinephilia was but one example of how graphic film violence was moving out of the arena of low culture and infiltrating other modes of film production. Even before the dismantling of the Production Code and the institution of the ratings system in the late 1960s, mainstream American filmmakers were pushing the violence envelope, albeit not to the extent of their filmmaking counterparts at the margins. While many filmmakers continued to use substitutional poetics (see Prince 2003) to varying degrees in order to obscure representations of violence, others ventured into more direct forms of representation. As Philip French notes, 'It [was] the form and intensity of violence that ... changed, rather than its quantity' (1968: 61). With more and more regularity, mainstream movie audiences saw blood squibs depicting the impact of bullets on bodies and other forms of bodily damage. For example, in *The Manchurian Candidate* (1962), the brainwashed Raymond Shaw (Laurence Harvey) shoots one of his fellow soldiers in the head onscreen (albeit in an extreme long shot), which is followed by a quick medium shot of a large amount of blood splattering a portrait of Josef Stalin behind the victim. In a torture sequence early in actor-director Cornel Wilde's bare-bones survival tale *The Naked Prey* (1966), a victim is stabbed just offscreen and a spurt of bright red blood shoots up into the frame, which may be the first example of arterial spray in an American film.[13] Not all such efforts towards making violence more gruesome actually made it to the screen, though, as can be seen in the case of Stanley Kubrick's *Spartacus* (1960), whose images of graphic violence (including a shot of Kirk Douglas chopping off an opposing warrior's arm, after which blood spurts from the stump) had to be shortened or eliminated to receive a Production Code Seal of Approval (see Prince 2003: 42) and to placate the Catholic Legion of Decency (see Black 1997: 214–15). Even in its trimmed version, *Spartacus* was a notably violent film, awash with 'barrels of bright red, fresh-from-the-paint-can blood', as the critic for *Time* magazine put it (Anon. 1960).

As for Hitchcock, he continued to push boundaries in *The Birds* (1963), which put even more blood on the screen than *Psycho* had and now in rich, luminous Technicolor. This time around Hitchcock employed his 'considerable skill' to orchestrate a series of vicious bird attacks, and no one is spared: not the heroine, Melanie Daniels (Tippi Hedren), not the elderly, and certainly not schoolchildren, a group of whom are the specific target in what is perhaps the film's most famous sequence. The relentless nature of the attacks and the rapid-fire editing that produces their fury contributes to the film's violent atmosphere, but it is the gory details that make them stick in the mind. The film's most visually shocking moment is when an elderly man is discovered dead in his bedroom with his eyes pecked out. Hitchcock draws us directly into the gruesome imagery with three rapid cuts, each of which brings us in closer until we are staring directly into the empty sockets. That same year Roger Corman directed *X: The Man With the X-Ray Eyes*, which ends with a shocking, if extremely brief close-up of the tragic hero, Dr James Xavier (Ray Milland), after he has torn his own eyes out.

The most important landmark in contemporary film violence arrived a few years later enmeshed in both controversy and acclaim: *Bonnie and Clyde*, Arthur Penn's bloody, comedic celebration of the counterculture, which exploded into the annals of cinema history with its climactic 22-second slow-motion machine-gun slaughter of the film's (anti)heroic couple (played by Warren Beatty and Faye Dunaway). However displeasurable that scene was for early audiences, Penn's stylistic rendering was undeniably innovative, conveying both 'the spastic and balletic qualities' (Crowdus & Porton 1994: 9) of violent death by combining various speeds of slow-motion with blood squibs to depict the physiology of bullet hits. Audiences had seen fleeting representations of exit wounds in earlier films such as Marlon Brando's *One-Eyed Jacks* (1961), but not in graphic motion and not with such a conflicting mixture of beauty and horror.

Bonnie and Clyde caused a significant rift among film critics, with the *New York Times*' Bosley Crowther railing against 'films of excessive violence [that] only deaden the sensitivities and make slaughter seem like a meaningless cliché' (1967a: 69), while the *New Yorker*'s Pauline Kael argued that *Bonnie and Clyde* contained 'a kind of violence that says something to us; it is something that movies must be free to use' (1968: 69). The divisive nature of the film is best illustrated by *Newsweek* critic Joe Morgenstern, who at first dismissed the film as a 'squalid shoot-'em for the moron trade', then wrote a second review in which he retracted his earlier response and argued for the necessity of distinguishing among types of cinematic violence (1968: 82).

The controversy heightened two years later with the release of Sam Peckinaph's *The Wild Bunch*, whose climactic battle between the eponymous outlaws and an entire Mexican army made *Bonnie and Clyde*'s death throes seem tame. Shot with as many as six Panavision, Mitchell and Arriflex cameras that were all running at different speeds with different wide angle, telephoto and zoom lenses (see Cook 1983: 123), the Agua Verde battle spans almost seven minutes and includes some 339 individual cuts. Critical reception of the film was mixed; at a contentious press conference following its unveiling to critics during a massive press junket in the Bahamas, some asked why the film had even been made while others hailed it as a masterpiece (see Anon. 1969).

In the mid- to late-1960s there was a series of cultural and industrial changes in the United States and Hollywood that all but guaranteed that direct representations of violence such as those in *Bonnie and Clyde* and *The Wild Bunch* would become the norm in mainstream films: the final dissolution of the Production Code and its replacement with the ratings system in 1968; the cultural climate change resulting from the Vietnam War, the Civil Rights movement and increasing public violence, all of which was mediated through television news; and the rising youth audience. These factors will be discussed at length in chapter four, where we will examine how the filmmakers of the New American Cinema depicted film violence and how that relates to the cultural and institutional changes of the era.

During the 1970s entire genres and subgenres built around violence included some of the most popular and, in some cases, critically acclaimed films of the decade: the vigilante film (*Dirty Harry*, 1971; *Walking Tall*, 1971; *Death Wish*, 1974; *Taxi Driver*, 1976); the disaster film (*Airport*, 1970; *The Towering Inferno*, 1974; *Earthquake*, 1974); and the horror film (*The Last House on the Left*, 1972; *The Exorcist*, 1973; *The Texas Chain Saw Massacre*; *Jaws*, 1975; *The Hills Have Eyes*, 1977; *Dawn of the Dead*, 1978; *Halloween*, 1978). Violence was also central to the emergence of a new trend known as blaxploitation, which included roughly sixty films released between 1969 and 1974 that 'generally consisted of a black hero out of the ghetto underworld, violently challenging "the Man" and triumphing over a corrupt, racist system' (Guerrero 2001: 214). Initially led by Melvin Van Peebles' fiercely independent *Sweet Sweetback's Baadasssss Song* (1971), which featured a powerful black protagonist who is radically politicised when he retaliates against racist violence inflicted by white police officers, the genre was slowly mainstreamed by Hollywood studios, which produced and distributed films such as *Shaft* (MGM, 1971), *Super Fly* (Warner Bros., 1973) and *Cleopatra Jones* (Warner Bros., 1973). However, as Ed Guerrero notes, although much of the violence in these films is of the 'fantastic popcorn' variety, it is still important because 'blaxploitation violence, in most cases, referenced black social reality, or transcoded, however fancifully, black political struggles and aspirations of the times' (ibid.).

The creation of the MPAA ratings system also allowed for the distribution of foreign-made films with substantial levels of violence such as *Straw Dogs*, *A Clockwork Orange* (1971), *Frenzy* (1972), *Flesh for Frankenstein* (1973), *The Street Fighter* and *Salò o le 120 giornate di Sodoma* (*Salò, the 120 Days of Sodom*, 1975), many of which directly interrogated the role of violence in society and in the cinema. Although at this time European cinema was more closely associated with depictions of sexuality than violence, there was nevertheless a significant rise in increasingly graphic horror films pouring out of Europe, especially Italian-made *gialli*, violent mystery-thrillers whose psychological themes of madness and paranoia are delineated with particularly baroque stylistic design and expressive use of music. Mario Bava led the way in the 1960s with films like *La ragazza che sapeva troppo* (*The Girl Who Knew Too Much*, 1963), in which a tourist witnesses a woman being stabbed to death and worries that she will be next, and *Sei donne per l'assassino* (*Blood and Black Lace*, 1964), in which six women are murdered in unique and sadistic ways, including one who is burned to death by having her face pressed against a red-hot stove. Bava was followed in the 1970s and 1980s by Dario Argento, who took the visual excesses of the *giallo* to new heights in films like *L'uccello dalle piume di cristallo* (*The Bird With the Crystal Plumage*, 1970), *Profondo rosso* (*Deep Red*, 1975), *Suspiria* (1977) and *Tenebre* (1982), mixing elements of fantasy and horror while orchestrating murderous violence with a rare intensity and operatic grandeur. As Maitland McDonagh notes, 'The voluptuousness of the murderous tableaux that are the centrepieces of Argento's works damns them doubly: they're distasteful both by virtue of their subject matter and in light of their technical prodigality' (1994: 23).

By the end of the 1970s, it is arguable that there was not much left to do with film violence that had not been done already. Thematically, the 1970s was incredibly rich in tying film violence to various ideological issues, whether it be the despair of urban decay and moral depravity in *Taxi Driver*, the absurdity of consumerism in *Dawn of the Dead*, or even the fundamental nature of human violence in *A Clockwork Orange*. Not surprisingly, all of these films were also on the forward edge of depicting violence in a brutally realistic manner, which was made possible by the innovations of make-up special effects artists like Tom Savini, Dick Smith, Rob Bottin, Stan Winston, Craig Reardon, Chris Walas and Tom Burman. While make-up effects artists had been celebrated in earlier decades as the men who created monsters, in the 1970s and 1980s they became pioneers in a new enterprise: the creative and, most importantly, realistic maiming of the human body. Thus, by the end of the decade, filmmakers had clearly established that visceral, graphic violence could be an important and accepted part of mainstream cinema.

Film violence in the 1980s and beyond

In contrast to the 1970s, when filmmakers were open and willing to use graphic depictions of violence to explore complex thematic issues, during the 1980s violent films were increasingly subjected to the Hollywood studios' commercial imperative to package film violence in ways that would take advantage of the audience's desire to be enthralled, rather than disturbed, by screen bloodshed (see Kendrick 2009). Thus, what differentiates the majority of film violence in the 1980s from the film violence employed in the late 1960s and much of the 1970s is the high-concept economic imperative that drove the majority of mainstream US film production during this era, regardless of genre or filmmaker intent. In contrast to the film violence of the 1970s, which was defended via appeals to the filmmaker's artistic vision and connections between the cinema and US society in the wake of the turbulent 1960s, violent films of the 1980s were insulated within a rhetoric of harmless, action-orientated escapism. The first years of the 1980s saw the end of the kind of complex, ambitious and potentially controversial violent films that had characterised the 1970s. Michael Cimino's *The Deer Hunter* (1978) and *Heaven's Gate* (1980), Francis Ford Coppola's *Apocalypse Now* (1979), Brian De Palma's *Dressed to Kill* (1980) and Martin Scorsese's *Raging Bull* (1980) gave way to violent films that were packaged as something completely different – mainstream, high-concept, audience-pleasing blockbusters like *Raiders of the Lost Ark* (1981), *Beverly Hills Cop* (1984), *Rambo: First Blood Part II*, *Top Gun* (1986) and *Batman* (1989). Film violence was just one of many components in the high-concept package explicitly designed to attract as many members of the most sought-after demographic as possible while simultaneously avoiding public controversy. There were, of course, exceptions, such as Ridley Scott's *Blade Runner* (1982), which used violence in a futuristic cityscape to question the very nature of humanity; David Lynch's *Blue Velvet* (1986), which depicted psychotic violence just beneath the placid façade of small-town Americana; the new spate of Vietnam films like Oliver Stone's *Platoon* and Stanley Kubrick's *Full Metal Jacket* (1987), which depicted combat with gory verisimilitude while critiquing the nature of war itself; Spike Lee's *Do the Right Thing* (1989), which depicted naked racial tensions on a hot summer day escalating into outright violence that audiences were forced to either condemn or condone; and even Paul Verhoeven's *RoboCop* (1987), which took a potentially silly science-fiction concept and escalated it with bloody black comedy and sharp jabs at capitalist excess.

As in the late 1960s, the changes in film violence in the 1980s were closely tied to larger changes in both American culture and the Hollywood industry. The 1980s was an era of increasing cultural conservatism, evinced by the back-to-back elections of Ronald Reagan as President and his immense build-up of the US military and its nuclear arsenal; the ascent of media-savvy religious groups such as Jerry Falwell's Moral Majority; and the national attention focused on money culture and so-called 'yuppies'. The socially conscious, disturbing and provocative violence that characterised so many films of the 1970s was being replaced by 'safer', though no less explicit forms of film violence.

This is not to say that there was not any controversy over the role of film violence in mainstream filmmaking. In fact, the 1980s was marked by a series of public battles over film violence waged by various grassroots organisations, film critics and government officials (see Lyons 1997). Although most of the violence in popular films of the 1980s fit the uncontroversial 'high-concept' mould, some filmmakers continued to push the envelope, particularly in the horror genre, which was all but taken over by 'slasher films' that were as popular as they were prolific in the wake of the enormous box-office success of *Halloween* and *Friday the 13th* (1980). The primary appeal of these films was creative murders depicted with explicit gore, and as a result they were immediately relegated to the bottom rung of the cultural ladder, despised by mainstream critics, some of whom, like the *Chicago Tribune*'s Gene Siskel, openly protested against them in print and on television. In the UK, slasher and other gory horror films, labelled 'video nasties' in the tabloid press, caused such a social panic in the early 1980s that the government passed the Video Recordings Act (VRA) in 1985 to restrict their distribution on home video.[14] The rhetoric around the new legislation centred on the protection of children, but it also functioned conveniently as a way for Members of Parliament to reassert their commitment to law and order in an election year and as a way for the culture as a whole to limit the influence of American and Italian films, which made up the bulk of those included on the 'video nasty' lists (see Kendrick 2004). Nevertheless, like the exploitation films and teenpics of the 1950s and 1960s, gory horror films, especially slasher films, were extremely popular with young audiences, who found thrills and humour in the simple formula of mysterious killer and nubile young victims.

Not all controversy over film violence was limited to low-budget horror films, though. In fact, some of the most public outcries were over films either produced or directed by Steven Spielberg, who had reached a pinnacle of critical and commercial success with *Jaws*, *Close Encounters of the Third Kind* (1977), *Raiders of the Lost Ark*, and *E.T.: The Extra-Terrestrial* (1982).

While Spielberg's reputation was that of a genial, family-friendly storyteller, especially in the wake of *E.T.*, his films consistently betrayed a darker sensibility and a willingness to interweave disturbing violence into the blockbuster mould. This was evident in *Jaws*, whose vivid depictions of people being attacked by a great white shark resulted in a special disclaimer that it may be 'too intense for young children' being added to the film's nonrestrictive PG rating in the US. *Raiders of the Lost Ark* featured an outrageous climax in which two Nazi villains' faces melt and another's head explodes, and the Spielberg-produced *Poltergeist* (1982) contained intense levels of fright and violence inflicted on children that caused a stir when the film was released with a PG rating. In the summer of 1984, *Gremlins*, produced by Spielberg, and *Indiana Jones and the Temple of Doom*, which he directed, finally pushed some over the edge, especially the latter's depiction of a sacrificial victim having his heart ripped from his chest. The Classification and Rating Administration responded by creating the PG-13 rating to categorise films between PG and R, the first and only addition to the ratings system since its inception in 1968.

Otherwise, throughout the 1980s film violence was seen more and more as a fully acceptable part of the medium, especially in action/spectacle films like *Commando*, *Cobra* (1986), *Lethal Weapon* (1987) and *Die Hard*, which depicted violence with bloody verisimilitude, but within a traditionally reactionary narrative framework that made for a pleasurable viewing experience. This carried over into the 1990s, in which there seemed to be a continuing escalation of violence in mainstream blockbuster films like *Die Hard 2: Die Harder* (1990), *Total Recall* (1990), *Terminator 2: Judgment Day* (1991) and *Basic Instinct*, as well as an explosion of so-called 'new violence', which was used to describe an emergent trend in art and independent films that mixed gore with over-the-top visual aesthetics and an ironic tone. By the early 1990s, B. Ruby Rich (1992) noted that the torch had officially passed in the indie film world from sex to violence.

The prime purveyor of this new violence in American cinema is Quentin Tarantino, whose *Reservoir Dogs*, *Pulp Fiction*, *Jackie Brown* (1996), *Kill Bill Vol. 1* (2003) and *Vol. 2* (2004), *Death Proof* (2007) and *Inglourious Basterds* (2009) openly borrow from and rewrite the traditions of film noir, blaxploitation, martial arts, action and war films within a framework of hip postmodernist pastiche. For Tarantino, violence is an aesthetic principle, one that can be freely manipulated and exploited in ways both serious and playful.

A grisly beating from one of the most violently divisive art-house movies of the period: *Irréversible* (2002)

His filmmaking approach opened the door for other similarly-minded film-makers, resulting in films like *Killing Zoe* (1994), directed by *Pulp Fiction* co-writer Roger Avary; *Lock, Stock, and Two Smoking Barrels* (1998), by British director Guy Ritchie; and *Desperado* (1995), directed by Robert Rodriguez, whose grindhouse sensibility led to several collaborations with Tarantino, including the criminals-on-the-lam/splatter-horror hybrid *From Dusk Till Dawn* (1996) and *Grindhouse* (2007), their relentlessly self-conscious ode to grimy 1970s exploitation cinema of which *Death Proof* was one-half of the 'double bill'. Tarantino and the filmmakers who, correctly or not, were seen as emulating his style emerged during a heady time for film violence that cut across national boundaries. In Belgium, the filmmaking team of Rémy Belvaux, André Bonzel and Benoît Poelvoorde created *C'est arrivé près de chez vous* (*Man Bites Dog*, 1993), a pseudo-documentary about a serial killer that is either a serious exploration of both filmmaking and the process by which spectators are implicated in viewing onscreen violence, or just a big, sick joke. In France, Gaspar Noé quickly became a controversial *cause célèbre* with his second feature *Irréversible* (2002), a divisive revenge story told in single takes structured in reverse chronological order. The film opens with a shockingly grisly depiction of the protagonist beating a man's head to a pulp with a fire extinguisher, although the film's controversy stemmed primarily from a gruelling eight-minute rape sequence that caused many to accuse the film of exploitation.

Thus, while some viewers saw profundity in this new art-house violence, others saw only emptiness, especially in Tarantino's films. As Steven
Gaydos, executive editor of *Variety*, put it, 'Quentin's stuff isn't really about
anything. It's comedic and self-referential. The classic Hollywood action
movies, [with] people like Peckinpah and Sam Fuller, were very political,
and quite profound. I think there's still ambivalence about Quentin's brand
of ultra-violence, devoid of any real gravity' (quoted in Bygrave 2003: 21).
Similarly, Stephen Prince has argued that this new violence, as embodied
in films like *Wild at Heart* (1990), *True Romance* (1993) and *Natural Born
Killers* (1994), is devoid of the moral gravity that gave weight to the films of
Sam Peckinpah: 'By adopting a dispassionate approach to ultraviolence,
contemporary films inoculate by numbing their viewers to the graphic dis-
plays of gore' (1998: 248). Such accusations are frequently levelled at Hong
Kong auteur John Woo, whose films *Dip huet seung hung* (*The Killer*, 1989)
and *Lat sau san taam* (*Hard-Boiled*, 1992) took the slow-motion montage
aesthetic pioneered by Kurosawa, Penn and Peckinpah to grandiose new
heights. This visual approach to violence was adopted by many Western
filmmakers, but when Woo was brought to the US, his style was initially
stymied by the Hollywood establishment. His American debut, *Hard Target*
(1993), was significantly re-edited to tone down both the explicit violence
and the director's more flamboyant cinematic tendencies, although they
were close to fully realised in his third Hollywood feature, *Face/Off* (1997).

Some have also argued that a handful of films in the 1990s did challenge viewers' preconceptions of film violence, and several long-standing
genres had new life breathed into them through either increasing the levels
of violence or questioning the very nature of violence, both cinematic and
real. The western had a brief resurgence in the early 1990s, culminating in
Clint Eastwood's *Unforgiven*, which withholds easy justification as a means
of questioning the redemptive and purgative violence that typically char-
acterises the genre (see Plantinga 1998). There was a also a cycle of films
that sought to interrogate the role of violence in African-American urban
ghettos, including John Singleton's *Boyz N the Hood* (1991) and the Hughes
brothers' *Menace II Society* (1993). While some critics championed these
films as drawing attention to the raw truths of the interconnections among
poverty, racism and black-on-black violence, others, such as Ed Guerrero,
have argued that 'in their violent nihilism (and sometimes self-contempt)
[they] hardly suggest the possibility of social change' (2001: 215). There

was also a resurgence in historical films that explored the depths of human violence, including *Schindler's List*, which was the first Hollywood studio film to take the Holocaust as its primary subject; *Rosewood* (1996), which depicted a neglected piece of twentieth-century history in which an all-black Florida town was destroyed by a white mob; and *Amistad* (1997), which portrayed a revolt on a slave ship and the subsequent trial to determine the escaped Africans' rights. The end of the 1990s also produced two notable films about World War Two: Steven Spielberg's *Saving Private Ryan* and Terrence Malick's *The Thin Red Line* (1998). While Spielberg opted to emphasise the audio-visual powers of the cinema to bring the ferocity of war to the audience in an unprecedented fashion, Malick chose to use the war film as a meditation on life, death and the destruction of the natural world. War also provided a template for David O. Russell's genre-defying war comedy *Three Kings* (1999), which took gun violence to a new level by showing interior views of the human body as bullets pass through vital organs.

The 2000s have seen all manner of film violence – graphic and subtle, exploitative and contemplative, serious and humorous. Many of the same trends that characterised the 1990s have persisted into the twenty-first century, including the popularity of blockbuster action movies that feature largely sanitised violence to thrill the audience and ensure big box office. The explosion of superhero films, most notably the *Spider-Man* trilogy (2001, 2004, 2007), *Batman Begins* (2005) and *The Dark Knight, Superman Returns* (2006), *Iron Man* (2008), *Watchmen* (2009) and the *X-Men* films (2000, 2002, 2004, 2009) have all engaged issues of film violence on varying levels, whether it be issues of justice and vigilantism in the *Batman* films or the repression of minorities in *X-Men*. On a darker note, the 2000s have witnessed a massive resurgence in horror films, especially remakes of 1970s classics such as *The Texas Chainsaw Massacre* (2003) and *The Hills Have Eyes* (2006), virtually all of which are grittier, gorier and more intense than even the most exploitative films of previous decades. Epitomised by the *Saw* (2004–) franchise and two *Hostel* films (2005, 2007), the development of so-called 'torture porn' has pushed the limits of mainstream film violence to a brink that would have been unthinkable even ten years ago. While this trend is currently on the downswing, the popularity of film violence in all its many manifestations continues, suggesting that it will always endure, as it has in other forms of art and entertainment, as long as real-life violence continues to define human history.

3 VIOLENCE AND GENRE: THE WESTERN, HORROR AND ACTION FILM

> All film genres treat some form of threat – violent or otherwise – to
> the social order.
>
> Thomas Schatz, *Hollywood Genres* (1981: 26)

As we have seen, violence is an essential component of the cinema,
part of the 'deep formal structure', as Stephen Prince (2003: 3) puts it.
Therefore, it only makes sense that it is also essential to film genre, which
has become the dominant means by which most viewers understand and
make sense of popular movies, especially within the organisational logic
of video stores and their online counterparts.

Even a cursory overview of genre movies, defined by Barry Keith Grant
as 'those commercial feature films which, through repetition and variation,
tell familiar stories with familiar characters in familiar situations' (1995:
xv), illustrates the importance of violence to both their underlying structure
and their ideological emphases. If, as Thomas Sobchack argues, 'the basic
principle of the genre film [is] the restoration of the social order' (1995:
112), then violence is implied on two fronts: in the initial destruction of the
social order and in its subsequent restoration. Violence of some kind is
the problem and, more frequently than not, also the solution. Horror and
science fiction films, action/adventure films, war films, westerns, mystery/
suspense and crime films, even many comedies and melodramas all rely
in some way on violence as a structuring device; thus, a focus on violence

presents a useful avenue for better understanding the historical development of these genres and how they function.

The centrality of violence is either implied or stated directly in many of the most influential scholarly writings on the subject of film genre. For example, Thomas Schatz argues that 'All film genres treat some form of threat – violent or otherwise – to the social order', and genres are distinguishable primarily by 'the attitudes of the principal characters and the resolutions precipitated by their actions' (1981: 26). Similarly, in 'Genre Films and the Status Quo', Judith Hess Wright (1995) argues that genres have clear and defined ideological agendas in which they raise fears about pertinent cultural subjects and then alleviate those fears by reasserting the status quo. Wright examines four genres – westerns, horror, science fiction and gangster films – and argues that violence is the key to understanding their ideology. For westerns, the central problem is how violence can be used, and the genre solves the problem by showing that violence is acceptable when used in a morally righteous way that respects an unchanging, masculine code of honour. Horror films centre on the conflict between rational/scientific and traditional means of problem solving and show that science ultimately cannot replace the traditional values and beliefs that are needed to kill the monster, the three-dimensional embodiment of evil. Similarly, science fiction films, especially those from the Cold War era, focus on how we can confront and ultimately destroy 'the Other'. And, finally, the gangster film, which deals with the necessity of competition in the capitalist enterprise, turns the gangster into a tragic hero who must die violently in the end because his ambition was too grand. In each instance, violence is both the problem and the answer, which neatly illustrates our moral and ideological ambivalence about it: violence is wrong only when it isn't serving our agenda. While many of Wright's arguments have been complicated and questioned since the piece was originally published in 1974, it is still a telling examination of the importance of violence to genre films and their ideological functioning. Even if violence is not as ideologically monolithic and unidirectional in meaning as Wright implies, it is nonetheless important.

One means of complicating the relationship between violence and genre is to consider the multiple levels of textual signification in genre films. A key strategy in this respect is Rick Altman's (1995, 1999) semantic/syntactic approach, which seeks to mediate the two primary, but conflicting theoretical approaches to genre: the ideological, in which genres are seen as manipulating the spectator (exemplified by the Wright article), and the ritual approach, in which genres are seen as reflecting spectator desire (exemplified by John Cawelti and Thomas Schatz's work, which emanates from the anthropological studies of Claude Lévi-Strauss). Drawing from a general theory of textual signification, Altman argues that film genres should be seen as being composed of semantic and syntactic elements. Semantic elements, which are equivalent to primary linguistic meaning, are the building blocks of the generic text (common traits, attitudes, characters, shots, locations and so on), while syntactic elements, which are equivalent to secondary textual meaning, are the thematic structures into which the semantic elements are organised. Therefore, a single phenomenon can have more than one meaning within a single film or across various films.

As an important semantic element in most film genres, violence has no inherent ideological meaning because said meaning will develop only in relation to how the violence is structured within the film's syntax. This lens allows us to look at different genres and consider the various ways in which violence is employed to both meet and undermine generic expectations. As Altman notes, 'We need to recognise that not all genre films relate to their genre in the same way or to the same extent. By simultaneously accepting semantic and syntactic notions of genre, we avail ourselves of a possible way to deal critically with differing levels of "genericity"' (1995: 33).

It is also important to recognise that genres are not static; rather, they are constantly evolving categories that are mutually agreed upon by filmmakers and film audiences. Genres are neither consistent nor transhistoric, but rather in constant flux, reflecting changes in both the state of the film industry and the socio-historical context in which they are produced. Numerous theories have been suggested to explain historical changes in film genres, one of the most well-known being Thomas Schatz's (1981) 'generic evolution', in which genres begin in transparency (straightforward storytelling) and move towards opacity (self-conscious formalism). Steve Neale views genre as a process in which 'the elements of a genre are always *in* play rather than being simply *replayed*' (1995: 170; emphasis in original). As we will see, the shifts in various genres and the differentiation within them often hinges on issues of violence: how it is depicted, what ideological function it serves, and so forth.

In this chapter, we will look briefly at three historically popular film genres that privilege violence as a semantic element – the western, the horror film and the action film – and consider the different ways in which violence is syntactically structured. Each genre will be treated somewhat differently because each is unique in its relationship to film violence. As we saw in chapter one, film violence is not a thing, but rather a complicated system of signifying practices that is understood by viewers as a subjective experience, and even though certain generic tendencies structure it in an attempt to enforce a particular reading, it can never be entirely contained within a set ideological system.

The western

An obvious place to start in any discussion of violence and film genre is the western, not only because this quintessentially American genre is fundamentally predicated on violence for its structure and meaning, but also because it was the focus of some of the earliest concentrated, book-length genre studies (for example, Cawelti 1971; Wright 1975). While much has been made about the iconographic elements of the western (the landscape, the costumes, six-shooters, horses, saloons), every study of this genre has also paid particular attention to the use of violence and its role in defining the western's relationship to issues of gender, society and law.

In the traditional or classic western (primarily those produced before the 1960s), violence is the chief means by which good and evil are distinguished. While the old adage suggests that the white hat denotes 'good' and the black hat denotes 'evil', the principal factor in distinguishing between the two is arguably *restraint*, particularly in the use of violence. Lee Clark Mitchell notes that the difference between heroes and villains in the western has less to do with ethics and morality than with 'an ability to resist giving way to inner desires and outer coercions' (2001: 180), one of which is the desire to use violence excessively (either when it is not needed or when it is used in a particularly brutal manner such as beating or stabbing with a knife). The western hero, who is almost always a man, actively resists such a desire: 'the cowboy hero does not seek out combat for its own sake and he typically shows an aversion to the wanton shedding of blood' (Cawelti 1984: 87). The villain, on the other hand, is a figure of excess in the western, deploying violence to satisfy his own desires; as Cawelti puts it, he 'delights in slaughter, entering into combat with a kind of manic glee to fulfil an uncontrolled lust for blood' (ibid.). This is, in every sense, illegitimate violence because it conflicts with the hero's code of restraint. Thus, if the hero is to use violence, then it must be seen as legitimate and 'pure', which necessitates that his violence be circumscribed.

Furthermore, the western hero's use of the six-shooter has significant implications for our attitude towards him. The ritual of the showdown and the ability of the hero to draw faster and take out the villain with one shot defines him in terms of 'reluctance, control, and elegance' (ibid.), which together form a particular masculine code of honour. The hero's quick-draw is a form of violence that is 'disciplined and pure', which is why the classic western hero never kills with his fists or by stabbing with a blade (1984: 88). Violence, then, is legitimate in the western only when it is used as a last resort, which is why so many of these stories culminate in a climactic showdown. As Cawelti suggests, the hero's reluctance to use violence and his emotional detachment when it is used gives 'a sense of moral significance and order to violence', masking its nakedness and aggression 'beneath a skin of aesthetic and moral propriety' (ibid.).

Yet, despite this avowed ethic that would seem to critique the use of force, the western is obsessed with violence. As Mitchell rightfully points out, the hero's restraint is less an ideal to admire than it is a means by which film violence can be deferred, thus increasing audience desire to see it. Mitchell points to *The Wild Bunch* as a film that reveals this manipulative tactic by opening with a visually assaultive sequence in which the titular outlaws blast their way out of a small town after holding up a railway station, causing the deaths (both directly and indirectly) of dozens of innocent bystanders in the process. By radically inverting the long-standing tradition of saving violence for the end, best exemplified by the lengthy build-up in *High Noon* (1952), Peckinpah 'expose[s] the rule's actual effect, which is less to encourage the impulse toward pacifism than to grant time to savour the imminence of violence that everyone knows will come' (2001: 187). At the end of *The Wild Bunch* Peckinpah again subverts expectations and exposes the artificial moral role violence had traditionally played in the genre. The film's climactic battle at Agua Verde is the very opposite of the traditional western's clean, aesthetically pure showdown: a chaotic and grotesque battle between the surviving members of the Bunch and an entire Mexican army, it exchanges the simple purity and precision of the six-shooter for the excessive force of a Gatling gun.

As the example of *The Wild Bunch* makes clear, the use of violence in the western was fundamentally altered in the late 1960s (as it was in many genres). The simple dichotomy of good violence (employed by the hero) and bad violence (employed by the villain) and the supposed virtues of restraint could no longer hold in an era defined by Vietnam, rising crime rates and public assassinations. However, there were important shifts in the genre well before *The Wild Bunch* and other revisionist westerns of the Vietnam era. As noted in chapter two, following World War Two the western departed significantly from its earlier incarnations. Lawrence Alloway attributes this at least partially to 'ageing stars (who needed more complex vehicles), intelligent writers, and conscientious directors', as well as 'an audience that had acquired as a result of war and/or college a knowingness about motivation and violence' (1971: 54).

While Alloway cites *Duel in the Sun* (1947) as giving the postwar western 'a massive injection of violence and sensuality' (ibid.), no film better embodied the genre's shift than John Ford's *The Searchers*, a landmark western that, in Thomas Schatz's words, was 'the most complex, critical, and evocative portrait of the West and the Westerner that movie audiences had yet seen' (1981: 72). The power of the film's underlying critique and reconsideration of the western's most fundamental themes is evinced by the strong influence it exerted on New American Cinema directors such as Steven Spielberg, Martin Scorsese and Paul Schrader, the latter of whom self-consciously used it as inspiration when writing *Taxi Driver*. The story concerns a years-long search for Debbie, a child who has been kidnapped by Comanches during a raid. Her uncle, Ethan Edwards (John Wayne), and a group of men set out to find her, but as the days turn to weeks and months and eventually years, everyone abandons hope except Ethan and Martin Pawley (Jeffrey Hunter), his brother's adopted part-Cherokee son.

Although we know little about Ethan's background, we do know that he is bitterly racist; his hatred for Indians is so intense that, during a shoot-out between Comanches and Texas Rangers, Ethan continues firing into the Indians' backs as they retreat, despite protests from the other men fighting by his side. Given his relentlessly violent nature, it is clear that the motives behind Ethan's drive to find Debbie are deep, complex and not always genuine. Although on its surface the film fits into the archetypal 'white man rescuing his woman from the savages' narrative, the film actually questions the very basis of that storyline. The entire search and its justification are turned upside down when we discover that Ethan does not want to save Debbie, but rather wants to kill her because she has been living peacefully with the Comanches as a squaw. Thus, Ethan rejects the traditional restraint of the western hero; in fact, his violence throughout the film is quite excessive, which aligns him with the traditional western villain. This is never more evident than when Ethan shoots out the eyes of a dead Comanche warrior just to spite him in the afterlife; although left offscreen, the violence is both gruesome in its wanton desecration of a corpse and also disturbing in what it tells us about the depths of hatred in Ethan's heart. His status as a loner, so typical of western heroes, is no longer romantic, but pathological.

This newly intensified violence in the postwar western was evident not just thematically, but also visually and stylistically, with bloodshed having more naturalistic detail and death having more physicality. In other words, westerns became bloodier in the 1950s, starting with *Ramrod* in 1947, which 'calibrated [violence] with a new precision: death by shotgun, protracted death after beating, callous shooting of an old man, and bloody faces after a slow-phased fistfight between heavyweights' (Alloway 1971: 54). At the same time, westerns became more obsessed with the weaponry of death, which was sometimes literalised in the films' titles (for example, *Winchester '73*, *Colt .45*, both 1950). There was also a marked focus on the intensified power of new weapons: the cannon in *The Battle of Apache Pass* (1952) and the Gatling gun in *Valiant* (1951) and *Siege of Red River* (1954) (see Alloway 1971; Leach 1975). Alloway attributes this emphasis on new and powerful weapons, as well as thematic attention paid to both their technological specificity and the moral issues involved in their usage, 'to audiences of veterans who had handled guns in World War Two and Korea', as well as 'the cold-war discussions of the period about arms standardisation for the NATO forces' (1971: 39).

This created an inevitable inclination towards challenging the previously accepted precepts of the genre, which turned into full-scale deconstruction in the late 1960s and early 1970s, especially in the wake of the brutal and existentially empty visions of the Italian spaghetti westerns. As Cawelti notes in 'Reflections on the Western Since 1970', a new chapter added to the second edition of *The Six-Gun Mystique*, films like *The Wild Bunch*, *Little Big Man* (1970), *McCabe and Mrs. Miller* (1971), *Pat Garrett and Billy the Kid* (1973) and *The Missouri Breaks* (1976) introduced such levels of moral ambiguity to the genre, especially in how violence was deployed, that they are best described as 'anti-Westerns'. As Cawelti notes, 'The Western hero's reluctance to initiate violence, and his "grace under pressure" seem archaic in an age of mass terror and potential nuclear catastrophe' (1984: 16).

Ralph Nelson's *Soldier Blue* (1970) is a particularly telling case study of how the use of violence in the western had fundamentally shifted in this era. *Soldier Blue* tells the story of a naïve young US Cavalry soldier, Honus Gent (Peter Strauss), travelling across Cheyenne territory with a young woman, Cresta (Candice Bergen), who has recently been 'rescued' from Cheyenne captivity, where she had lived for several years. The film self-consciously inverts many of the western's most cherished tropes as a means of critiquing the genre's underlying ideologies, especially as they involve the 'legitimate' use of violence. However, the film's ultimate focus on the violent subjugation of Native American populations by the US military is not entirely new. In fact, such subject matter was typical of pre-1910 films that have been retroactively labelled 'westerns', but arguably constituted their own genre of 'Indian films', which regularly featured 'noble "red men" mistreated by dissolute "whites"' (Altman 1999: 36). Similarly, the post-World War Two era included a number of films such as *Fort Apache* (1948), *The Devil's Doorway* (1950), *Sitting Bull* (1954) and *Run of the Arrow* (1957) whose thematic focus was on 'the untrustworthiness of whites' (Alloway 1971: 54). However, none of those films depicted the US military's hostile treatment of Native Americans with the graphic intensity evident in *Soldier Blue*, which is reflected in its marketing campaign as 'The Most Savage Film in History'.

Soldier Blue was one of a number of westerns made in the early 1970s that indirectly referenced the war in Vietnam and conflated it with the American conquest of the West and the related violence inflicted upon Native Americans, thus critiquing the 'exceptionalist' mythology of America. These films visualised the argument advanced by Richard Slotkin (1973) that the American exceptionalist myth and its related celebration of westward movement actually functions as a historical rationale for the violence of imperialism, class division, industrialisation and, most importantly, the systematic genocide of Native Americans. Ralph Nelson stated that he first gained interest in *Soldier Blue* when he saw his children learning American history that was distorted to celebrate the conquering of the West and erase the officially sanctioned violence perpetrated by the US Army against Native Americans (see 1970: 26). Thus, in making *Soldier Blue* one of the goriest mainstream American films at that time, Nelson sought specifically to redress the American exceptionalist mythology of westward expansion by bringing to the forefront the required – and often viciously excessive – violence that was levelled against native populations.

That *Soldier Blue* is a thinly disguised allegory of atrocities committed by US soldiers in Vietnam and the general oppression of the South Vietnamese people was noted by many critics at the time of its release. The film's climactic massacre of a Cheyenne village was modelled on both the Sand Creek Massacre in Colorado in 1864 and various atrocities committed by American troops in Vietnam, most notably the My Lai Massacre of 16 March 1968, and the Pinkville Massacre, which was exposed in the American press at the same time Nelson was researching for the film (see Nelson 1970). The intense levels of violence in *Soldier Blue* surpassed anything that had been seen in a major American film, including *Bonnie and Clyde* and *The Wild Bunch*. The massacre sequence includes graphic depictions of US Cavalry soldiers decapitating a Cheyenne mother, shooting a child through the eye and stripping a woman and proceeding to rape her. Throughout the sequence Nelson fills the screen with images of wanton death and destruction, including children with their limbs cut off and a woman's naked, bloody body strung up on a pole. The sequence culminates with the soldiers dancing around with various body parts – heads and arms and legs – skewered on the ends of their swords like trophies.[1]

The climactic massacre that divided audiences and critics: *Soldier Blue* (1970)

On the question of whether such graphic violence was necessary and justified for Nelson to make his point, opinion was sharply divided. S. K. Oberbeck, the critic for *Newsweek*, complained that 'the picture seems merely an excuse for rubbing our noses in the massacre' and 'the horror, even though historically authentic, becomes more symbolic than real' (1970: 65). Moira Walsh of *America* argued that the film was only 'pretend[ing] to decry violence' because it had 'been structured to appeal mainly to the unspeculative fan of violence' (1970: 186). And Margaret Ronan, writing in *Senior Scholastic*, wrote, 'But this movie *isn't* presented as truth for its own sake, just violence for the sake of kicks. It is an exploitation of history, not a re-creation' (1970: 20; emphasis in original). However, several critics applauded Nelson's use of graphic violence to make his point, which emphasises just how complex a matter it is justifying the use of graphic violence onscreen. In his lengthy defence of the film in the *New York Times*, Dotson Rader argued that 'the last portion of the film has been criticised for being too brutal, too honest. I do not think that it went far enough' (1970: 13). Similarly, in the British film journal *Films and Filming*, Peter Buckley wrote:

Which brings us to the valid question of 'Is this excess justified?' I say definitely yes. It does arise from the story and is the climax, almost the natural outcome of all that has gone before. The parallels drawn between the Sand Creek slaughter and current immoral American activities is relevant and even underlined, but they are secondary within *Soldier Blue*, as are any messages concerning militarism, racism and pacification within the framework of the film. Although we all know that war is a brutalising, numbing experience, it is a lesson we cannot be told too often. (1971: 66)

In the wake of *Soldier Blue* and other revisionist westerns of the 1970s (as well as parodies like Mel Brooks's *Blazing Saddles* (1974)), the western genre lost much of its ideological power. Violence had been fully exposed as the genre's primary preoccupation, and the rituals that had previously ordered 'good' violence and distinguished it from 'bad' violence no longer held sway. This is best epitomised in Clint Eastwood's *Unforgiven*, which deconstructs the hard-edged persona Eastwood had perfected in so many westerns during the 1960s and 1970s. Unlike classic westerns in which the hero's code of honour helped absolve the audience from vicariously enjoying the violent spectacle, *Unforgiven* withholds such justification, presenting us with a morally complicated central character whose violent gunplay at the end of the film, 'far from regenerative, is sinister and infectious – a sign of loss and failure' (Plantinga 1998: 79). However, as Carl Plantinga points out, the film nevertheless 'satisfied the spectator's desire for the dramatic violent purge and emotional release by granting the hero his killing, however ambiguously represented' (ibid.). Yet, as John Cawelti (1984) noted several years before *Unforgiven* was produced, it is the very introduction of ambiguity into the western that essentially destroys its ideology of regeneration through necessary, morally defensible violence. Thus, *Unforgiven* could very well be, in Chuck Berg's words, 'the western's last will and testament' (2000: 219).

Even when regenerative violence is enacted in more contemporary films like Kevin Costner's *Open Range* (2004), the closest a recent Hollywood production has come to a traditional western, its 'purity' is purposefully compromised both thematically and aesthetically. The violence of the film's final showdown between free grazers Boss Spearman (Robert Duvall) and Charlie Waite (Costner) and a gang of thugs hired by a corrupt cattle baron is often awkward and unanticipated, in no way resembling the clean, aesthetically pleasing violence of traditional westerns. The gunfighters are a mix of novices and experts, and Costner prefaces the shoot-out with a monologue in which his character predicts how the various men will react. Unlike so many western movie shoot-outs, not everyone stands his ground or does exactly what the genre would typically dictate. Rather, some men cower, some act bravely and others make mistakes. It is a strong rejection of classical western violence, substituting complexity and ambiguity for grace and purity.

The horror film

Given the extraordinarily gory and sadistic nature of so many contemporary horror films, with their onslaught of realistically rendered blood spurts, torn flesh, severed limbs and mutilated bodies, it might seem to the casual filmgoer that violence and the horror genre are not just connected, but fundamentally, ontologically inseparable. Clearly, violence of some kind, even if understood as simply the *threat* of violence, is absolutely essential to the horror genre; otherwise, there would be no suspense and no reason to fear the film's threat, whether it be human or supernatural. As Gregory A. Waller notes, 'Taken as a whole, the entire [horror] genre is an unsystematic, unresolved exploration of violence in virtually all its forms and guises' (2000: 260). Yet, the relationship between violence and horror as a genre has long been a contested issue, especially how the violence is visualised. Simply put, does horror violence need to be visually graphic, that is, *gory*?

Many scholars have argued against the need for graphic verisimilitude in representing onscreen violence in horror films, while others have argued that it is essential to the genre because part of the essence of cinematic horror is the transgression of visual taboos. Such arguments about the explicitness of horror violence are inherently ideological because, more often than not, they correspond to conventional high/low cultural divides. 'Suggestive' or 'indirect' horror films – those that rely on the interplay of light and shadow, foreboding music, canted camera angles and other traditional means of generating suspense – are considered more 'highbrow', whereas those horror films that revel in visually graphic representations of violence, especially the 'slasher' films spawned in the wake of *Friday the 13th*, are considered 'lowbrow' and disreputable because they address the body directly, rather than the mind. As Waller points out, the celebration of indirect, non-graphically violent horror is often associated with 'a nostalgic longing for the "golden age" of horror' (2000: 261), although, as we saw in chapter two, films like *Dracula* and *Frankenstein*, while seemingly benign now, caused serious consternation among moviegoers and social reform groups at the time of their release.

Two of the seminal early histories of the horror genre, Carlos Clarens' *An Illustrated History of Horror and Science-Fiction Films* (1967) and Ivan Butler's *Horror in the Cinema* (1971), take a generally disparaging view towards graphic violence, which was a relatively new phenomenon at the time of their writing, but has since become one of the genre's defining characteristics. Clarens' intense focus on the mythical-poetic dimensions of horror effectively disassociates direct violence from the genre, at least in its most artistically satisfying manifestations. Clarens concedes that horror has a violent dimension and notes that a 'supremely violent age like ours calls for unprecedented violence in its aesthetic manifestations' (1967: xix), yet he tends to view violence as detracting from horror's 'myth, tradition, and legend' (1967: 37). For example, in his critical assessment of Hammer

Films' 1958 version of *Dracula*, Clarens notes that, because the film takes the approach of having 'all scenes swimming in a wealth of gory detail', it 'failed where the others had at best made something of themselves, in the evocation of a timeless, intangible evil' (1967: 142). In other words, an incessant focus on the physical detracts from any spiritual or mythical themes, which are inevitably considered more culturally worthwhile (see Paul 1994). Ivan Butler is quite explicit in his assertion that indirect horror is aesthetically superior and more effective than direct horror when he writes 'the unseen is often more frightening than the seen' (1971: 13). While he is writing primarily about the monster and how much it should be revealed, it is not hard to extend this logic to depictions of violence and whether they should be front and centre or left offscreen. Butler goes on to suggest that the audience (at least his presumed audience, which is composed of spectators of 'normal sensibility') is inherently turned off by films that revel in sadism and beastliness (see 1971: 18).

Nevertheless, graphic horror violence has become one of the genre's central elements, beginning in the 1960s and reaching a mainstream apotheosis in the subgenre of so-called torture porn, which includes the *Saw* series, *The Devil's Rejects* (2005), *Wolf Creek* (2005) and *Hostel* and *Hostel Part II*, as well as the more graphic remakes of 1970s films like *The Texas Chain Saw Massacre* and *The Hills Have Eyes*. However, this subgenre seems to have lost much of its popularity, which suggests that one way to view graphic horror violence is as a cyclical element in the genre that is not essential, but is not necessarily something to be shunned either. We can see gore as a semantic generic element that can be and has been used to varying degrees at different points in the horror genre's cycle. In his book *The Thrill of Fear: 250 Years of Scary Entertainment* (1991), Walter Kendrick argues that the increasingly explicit gore in horror films is not inherent to the genre, but is rather a means of refreshing it, which makes sense in relation to torture porn given that these films followed a wave of significantly less violent, spiritually orientated horror films like *The Sixth Sense* (1999), *Stir of Echoes* (1999), *The Gift* (2000) and *The Others* (2001). Increasingly graphic violence was used in the late 1950s as a way of bringing the horror genre back to life after it had nearly been killed off by a flurry of self-parodic films best exemplified by the *Abbott and Costello Meet...* series, which included *Frankenstein* (1948), *Dr. Jekyll and Mr. Hyde* (1953) and *The Mummy* (1955). As noted in chapter two, the horror movies produced by Hammer Films in the 1950s resurrected the monsters of the 1930s Universal horror series with Technicolor blood and a newfound willingness to focus directly on ghastliness and gore, rather than discreetly cutting away. These films, along with a series of US-made films of the same era such as *Macabre* (1958), *Psycho*, *Blood Feast* and *Night of the Living Dead*, formed the one discernible trend in horror filmmaking of the past four decades: the rising explicitness of gore.

Kendrick is in a somewhat ambivalent position because he admits that he does not particularly care for graphic violence, yet, in defending the horror genre as a meaningful cultural product, he must justify it in some way given its pervasiveness. To bridge this divide, he discusses graphic violence in relation to the horror audience, which, rather than being composed of Ivan Butler's spectators of 'normal sensibility', is instead a tightly bound group 'who makes a cult of the whole business and revels in arcane information that only fellow fans share' (1991: 255). Horror films since the 1960s have become 'specialised products aimed at audiences that know what to expect and what is expected of them' (1991: 251); thus, graphic violence functions as a means of maintaining solidarity within horror fandom while keeping out those who do not have it in them to appreciate the technical wizardry and perverse artistry of creatively maiming the human body through special effects.

Similarly, Mark Kermode sees the horror genre as feeding on the knowledge of its fans, who are able to appreciate graphic horror violence because they can read it both metaphorically and as a product of creativity, rather than simply taking it at face value. Kermode suggests that there is an 'absolute divide between horror fans and everyone else in the world' (1997a: 59) that is predicated on the fans' knowledge-induced appreciation of the genre and its violence. The taboo aspect of graphic violence – the way it allows us to see what is normally hidden and reflect on the fragility (and grossness) of our own bodies – is key to the appeal of watching gory horror movies, even though viewers understand it as a constructed fiction to which they willingly subject themselves and their insecurities. Because horror fans are well-versed in the behind-the-scenes work of writers, directors and special effects artists – initially through books and fan magazines such as *Fangoria*, but increasingly through supplementary material on DVDs – they understand horror violence 'in terms of a heritage of genre knowledge', while nonfans are repulsed because they cannot 'see past the special effects, puncture the gaudy surface of the movies, pull apart their rubbery rib-cages and grasp their dark thematic hearts' (1997a: 61). While Kermode understates the taboo sadistic pleasures some fans may get from watching onscreen bloodshed, he is right in noting that they are also able to recognise that horror violence addresses various thematic concerns, which allows them to distinguish between serious and satirical violence. Fans are able to recognise the inherent silliness of the gore in *The Evil Dead* (1982) and therefore delight in both the low-budget innovation of the gore effects and the references to *Three Stooges*-style slapstick comedy; at the same time, though, they recognise the cultural, racial and social issues in *Night of the Living Dead* or the serious psychological dimensions of John McNaughton's *Henry: Portrait of a Serial Killer*. In this way, horror violence can be seen as both inclusive, in that it helps bring together a community of fans who appreciate what the genre has to offer, and exclusive in the way it aggressively repels those who do not.

Another way to look at horror is to consider the functional relationship between film violence and the genre's ideological implications. The question of whether the horror genre is an essentially reactionary or transgressive genre is one that has been at the centre of the study of horror for many years, particularly since the 1970s when scholars turned to psychoanalytic and Marxist cultural approaches to better understand how films work on audiences and how they affect and are affected by social norms. As we have already noted, violence is a fundamental semantic element of the horror genre, and how it is used syntactically is crucial to understanding a particular film's positioning along the ideological spectrum.

Some scholars, like Judith Hess Wright (1995), have argued that the horror genre and its violence serve a primarily conservative/reactionary function. On the other hand, Robin Wood (1996) has argued that the horror genre, at least in its post-1960s incarnations, is frequently transgressive in the way it brings to the surface everything that patriarchal capitalist ideology seeks to repress, primarily issues of sexuality and our relationship with various 'Others', which can be loosely defined as anything that is not heterosexual white and male (women, children, homosexuals, different racial and ethnic groups and so on). 'Transgressive', in this sense, refers to the genre's ability to break down boundaries, rupture binaries and disrupt order and easy categorisation. We can see this at work in films such as *Night of the Living Dead* and *The Texas Chain Saw Massacre*, which do not conclude with simple reassertions of the status quo (the very definition of a reactionary/conservative narrative). *Night of the Living Dead* is a particularly intriguing example in that the status quo *is* ironically reasserted via the killing of the black lead character by a white posse who – maybe – think he is a zombie, which self-consciously brings the racial ideology behind such a violent conclusion into question.

We can also consider the relationship between horror violence and ideology through the lens of gender, which has been a particularly vexed issue due to horror's historically relentless assault on women and subsequent criticisms by those who see the genre as inherently misogynistic. One of the most oft-cited assertions about the horror film is that it is structured around male violence against female victims, an argument that seems to be illustrated again and again by images of shrieking, terrified women cowering from a physically masculine monstrosity. This tendency in the genre took a particularly nasty bent in the 1970s and 1980s when the slasher film, with its knife-wielding killer stalking and slaughtering predominantly female victims (often following a sexual encounter), was at the zenith of its popularity. Such a scenario gives the impression that the horror genre is rabidly reactionary, punishing illicit sexuality and constantly victimising women as a way of asserting male dominance both visually and physically. However, a number of scholars have argued for the genre's fundamentally contradictory nature, particularly in relation to its use of gendered violence.

Rhona J. Berenstein (1996) has challenged a number of gender-related assumptions about the horror film, including the idea that the genre is structured around an inherently sadistic male gaze. Similarly, Linda Williams (1984) has argued that, while women are victimised by the gaze of horror monsters, there is also a connection between them as outsiders within patriarchal societies. Carol Clover (1992) has demonstrated quite persuasively that slasher films, the most abhorred subgenre of horror, are not as simplistic and misogynistic as their critics like to attest. For Clover, violence is essential to the horror genre because it creates victims, identification with whom is central to the genre's effect. The audience, which is assumed to be predominantly young and male, is encouraged to identify with the so-called 'Final Girl', who ultimately appropriates the violence of the gender-confused slasher and kills him. Thus, the violence in such films creates female protagonists 'in the full sense: they combine the functions of suffering victim and avenging hero' (1992: 17). The Final Girl's eventual triumph depends entirely on her assuming the film's gaze, which is often conflated with violence and control, especially through the use of the subjective camera to see through the killer's eyes, which many critics have taken as proof of the genre's inherently sadistic and masculine identification. However, while the Final Girl is clearly designated as a victim and suffers accordingly, rather than simply providing sadistic visual pleasure for the audience, these actions also encourage viewers to identify with a female surrogate onscreen, an act that challenges the assumption that male viewers can only identify with male characters.

As these examples suggest, when thinking about the ideological role of violence in the horror film, it is a mistake to think of the genre as being either inherently transgressive or inherently reactionary. As Berenstein notes, to do so 'oversimplifies one of its most important qualities; namely, its function as a site of ideological contradiction and negotiation' (1996: 10). With this in mind, we can see the violence of the horror genre functioning along an ideological continuum, with some films expressing more reactionary tendencies through their violence, while others deploy violence for explicitly transgressive purposes, and others are hopelessly muddled. To explore a bit further, we might consider the various ways in which horror violence can be shaped narratively, tonally and visually to either reactionary or transgressive ends.

In terms of narrative, we can look at who uses violence and for what purpose. In its reactionary role, violence tends to be wielded by evil monsters and conventional symbols of patriarchal authority such as male scientists, police officers and soldiers. This kind of violence marks a clear divide between 'good' and 'evil', which is similar to violence's function in the western. The role of the monster is crucial in this regard because, as Wood (1996) has noted, the monster often functions metaphorically, and when it is seen as unproblematically evil and deserving of absolute destruction, it evokes similar feelings towards the socially marginalised the monster often represents. However, some horror films show violence being used by monsters that are not so transparently evil; while still monstrous (otherwise, how could he/she/it be scary?), there are elements to the character that might arouse pity or sympathy. One of the best examples is James Whale's *Frankenstein*, in which the monster kills a young girl (in a scene that was frequently censored during its initial theatrical release), but is still depicted as sympathetic, even victimised. A horror film can also show masculine power to be impotent, which is frequently the case in slasher movies that feature masked killers acting out psychosexual aggression and ultimately being killed by a Final Girl, as well the various boyfriends, police officers and other male 'saviours' who consistently fail in their efforts to save her (see Clover 1992).

Violence can also be made transgressive in terms of its tone, especially when graphic violence and comedy are mixed because it encourages the audience to laugh at that which should not be funny. There is a reticence on the part of many people to admit that graphic violence can be humorous because it seems so inappropriate, which is why laughing at such imagery is inherently transgressive of social norms. More conservative horror films tend to take their violence seriously, whether it is explicit or indirect. On the other hand, the mixing of comedy and violence, especially graphic gore, in films like *Re-Animator* (1985), *Evil Dead II* (1987) and *Braindead* (aka *Dead-Alive,* 1992) breaks down the boundaries between the 'serious' and the 'humorous' and also draws our attention to how virtually all comedy is based on violence, whether it be physical slapstick or verbal putdowns. Gory horror comedies invite their viewers to laugh out loud at physical dismemberment and other bodily mutilations, and in this sense are perfect distillations of the inherent complexities of defining an act as 'violent' (if it's funny, is it still violent?).

Finally, horror violence can be transgressive in a purely visual sense, hence the long-running debate about the place of graphic violence in the genre. When horror violence is graphic – when it exploits the affective nature of the cinema and makes involuntary physical response the primary mode of reception – it transgresses polite cultural norms by exposing that which should be hidden, which threatens the proper social order (see Paul 1994). It also blurs the boundary between text and viewer by inducing physical effects in the spectator's body such as nausea, abdominal discomfort, muscle tension and even vomiting. In a culture that holds restraint and decorum as high moral standards, inviting such responses is not socially acceptable. It immediately codes violent horror films as a low form of culture, similar to melodrama and pornography (see Williams 1995), and, when taken to extremes in films such as *Snuff* (1976) and *Cannibal Holocaust* (1980), encourages social panic and censorship (see Brottman 2005).

To conclude, we will look at one horror film, *Flesh for Frankenstein*, and examine its use of graphic violence as a way to illustrate how this semantic genre element can function both conservatively and transgressively within the same film. The film's director, Paul Morrissey, was a member of Andy Warhol's Factory, but was the lone conservative of the group who detested the arty pretences of his contemporaries and refused to work with anyone using drugs (see Yacowar 1993). Thus, it is not surprising that *Flesh for Frankenstein*'s ideological agenda was largely reactionary, offering a sharp critique of excess in any form, particularly meaningless sexual excess. At the same time, though, the film can be read as transgressive, partially because its liminal status as both an avant-garde art film and a delirious gross-out horror-comedy directly negates the high/low culture divide (see Hawkins 2000).

The film is visually transgressive, with an explicit focus on guts and gore – ranging from numerous, almost fetishistic disembowelments, to hands being cut off, to impalements – all of which was heightened with the parodic use of Space-Vision, a polarised 3-D process, to literally dangle intestines and a skewered spleen in the viewer's lap. The film delights in sordid grossness and asks viewers to laugh even though (or because) they are repulsed. Yet, despite the visually transgressive nature of the film's ludicrously graphic violence, the narrative is deeply conservative, retroactively critiquing the kind of sexual excess that was endemic of 1960s counterculture. This is seen most clearly in the incestuous relationship between the Baron (Udo Keir) and the Baroness (Monique van Vooren), which has resulted in the birth of two creepy, near-mute children, thus suggesting that deviant family practices produce deviant children. The fact that the Baron and Baroness's relationship is depicted as a parody of the traditional American family would seem to be the kind of transgressive critique of dominant ideology seen in *The Texas Chain Saw Massacre* and *The Hills Have Eyes*, but the fact that both characters are severely punished for their carnal excess suggests that Morrissey is up to something else.

In *Flesh for Frankenstein*, the connection between sex and violent death is omnipresent: every character dies not only as a direct result of some form of deviant sexuality, but often *in the very act*. The first character to die is Sacha (Srdjan Zelenovic), an innocent young man who wants to be a priest and is mistakenly beheaded by the Baron, who thinks he is sexually promiscuous and therefore wants his brain for the male zombie

The transgressive function of violence: *Flesh for Frankenstein* (1973)

he is making in his laboratory. Olga (Liu Bosisio), the family's maid, is the next to die, disembowelled by the Baron's assistant, Otto (Arno Juerging), during a sexual assault. Otto later kills the Baron's female zombie (Dalila Di Lazzaro) when he tries to engage with her sexually as the Baron had earlier, but ends up disembowelling her as well. The Sacha zombie crushes the Baroness to death in his arms when she forces him to have sex with her and later impales the Baron with a spear, after which he commits suicide by disembowelling himself because he cannot stand to go on in his current state. And, while Nicholas (Joe Dallesandro), the film's most sexually care-free character, is technically left alive at the end, hanging by his arms in the Baron's lab, the slow descent of the Baron's children with scalpel in hand is a sure sign of his impending doom. Thus, the film's violence functions conservatively on a narrative level by explicitly connecting sexual excess with violent punishment, but transgressively on a visual level by blurring the boundaries between art film and gross-out horror and asking the audience to laugh at imagery that would repulse polite society.

The action film

Of the three genres discussed in this chapter, the action film is the most recently developed, as it did not cohere into a recognisable independent category until the past few decades. Prior to the 1970s, when Eric Lichtenfeld argues that the heroes of the action film genre were 'liberated from the for-eign battlefields and distant pasts to which they had often been consigned' (2004: xv), 'action film' was more of an umbrella term under which more specifically recognisable genres were loosely grouped. For example, in Lawrence Alloway's companion book to 'The American Action Movie: 1946–1964', a film series he and several others organised at New York's Museum of Modern Art in 1969, he rarely uses the term 'action film' and instead categorises films more specifically as 'westerns', 'gangster films', 'war films' and so on, suggesting that action is but one semantic element that can be easily contextualised within multiple genres. Three decades later, *Sight & Sound* published a reader titled *Action/Spectacle Cinema* (Arroyo 2000) that includes discussions of fantasy (*Hook*, 1991), horror (*Bram Stoker's Dracula*, 1992), crime (*Pulp Fiction*; *Heat*, 1995) and science fiction (*Demolition Man*, 1993; *Starship Troopers*, 1997; *The Matrix*), as well as those films that are generally considered 'pure action' in that action spectacle is their primary draw and they have no other immediate generic connections (*Bad Boys*, 1995; *Die Hard With a Vengeance*, 1995; *The Long Kiss Goodnight*, 1996). Thus, while little has changed in terms of the affinity of 'action' with other long-standing genres, a major difference is that now a film like *The Matrix* is just as likely to be referred to as an action film as a science fiction film. Action has become a dominant mode of discourse in film genre.

There have been elements of the action film in the cinema since its beginnings. In fact, action is such a fundamental part of the cinema that it is difficult to separate the two. The early history of film aesthetics is largely the history of filmmakers innovating better means of representing movement and increasing the intensity of the viewing experience through continuity editing, camera movement and special effects. It is not incidental that one of the most important developments in the nascent cinematic language was the French *course comique* or comic chase films, which were extremely popular at the turn of the twentieth century and were instrumental in constructing synthetic space through editing, as well as subverting all narrative to the subsequent chase – the action (see Abel 1994). So, in these rudimentary chase films we have the underlying ethos of the action film as it now stands. Of course, the action in these comic chase films is fairly benign in the sense that they usually include a pursued and pursuers surmounting various obstacles in a comic fashion with little threat of bodily injury or dire consequence at the end.

However, this should not blind us to the fact that the word *action* when used in a cinematic context is little more than a euphemism for *violence* that does not carry the latter's negative connotations. *Action* is excitement, movement and velocity, while *violence* suggests something unauthorised, unruly, even vehement and vulgar. Action enthralls, violence violates, which is why the protagonists of action films are referred to as 'action heroes', rather than 'violent heroes', even though the latter is as apt a description, perhaps more so. It should come as little surprise that the aforementioned 1969 film series at the Museum of Modern Art was originally organised under the title 'Violent America: The Movies 1946–1964', but the title was changed to 'The American Action Movie' under protest from one of the film companies lending a print (see Alloway 1971: 7).

Prior to recent decades, when the term *action* was used to denote a genre it was usually conjoined with *adventure*. As a marketing tool, this dates back to at least the late 1920s when *Film Daily* used it to describe the Douglas Fairbanks film *The Gaucho* (1927), and it reached its peak of popularity in the 1930s and 1940s with films like *Captain Blood* (1935), *The Adventures of Robin Hood* (1938), *The Thief of Bagdad* (1940) and *The Sea Wolf* (1941). According to Steve Neale (2000), action/adventure films have several common characteristics: spectacular physical action; narrative emphasis on fights, chases and explosions; and the use of special effects and stuntwork. They also tend to centre around spectacular male bodies on display, from the lean and muscular physiques exhibited by Fairbanks and Tyrone Power in the 1920s, 1930s and 1940s, to the muscle-bound 'hard bodies' of the 1980s exemplified by Arnold Schwarzenegger and Sylvester Stallone (see Jeffords 1994). Thus, like the western, the action film is a predominantly male genre that uses violence to provide appealing, if unrealistic models of masculine power.

In the late 1970s there was a decided shift in action/adventure movies with the emergence of what Larry Gross (2000) calls 'the Big Loud Action Movie', which has several distinguishing characteristics: the use of simplistic B-movie plots, the reduction of narrative complexity, the domination of the narrative by image and technology, and self-deprecating humour. In sum, these characteristics involve the recession of narrative, theme and character and the elevation of the purely sensational, which is why violence is so crucial to both the form and meaning of these films. Different scholars have argued for different starting points for this kind of action film in which everything is ultimately subservient to spectacle; as Thomas Leitch puts it, 'The roots of the action film remain in Aristotelian dramaturgy; what twentieth-century cinema adds is a change in emphasis that substitutes spectacular elements – not only of action as such, but of many particular associations of action – for the teleological, ethically consequential associations central to Aristotle' (2004: 109). Eric Lichtenfeld marks the beginnings of the modern action film in the early 1970s when films like *The French Connection* (1971), *Shaft* and *Dirty Harry* combined the urban landscape of film noir, detective and gangster films with the classic western conflicts between the law and lawlessness, but with an exaggerated emphasis on the violent elimination of the villain. The most oft-cited turning point in terms of spectacular action is the work of George Lucas and Steven Spielberg in the late 1970s and early 1980s, specifically *Star Wars* and *Raiders of the Lost Ark*, both of which are self-consciously heightened throwbacks to earlier cinematic forms. Larry Gross also notes the importance of the James Bond series, particularly the shift in which 'espionage and plot mechanics disappear almost entirely' in favour of 'an entirely new super-kinetic cartoon-type action movie' exemplified by *Goldfinger* (1964) and *Thunderball* (1965) (2000: 5).

The James Bond series, which at the time of this writing includes 22 'official' films spanning more than 45 years with six different actors in the lead role, offers a useful case study of the action genre because the films have been so influential in shaping the nature of action violence in the contemporary movie marketplace. The immense popularity of Bond films around the world and across more than four decades shows that their brand of formulaic action violence and excessive spectacle speaks across cultural, geographic and temporal divides. In many ways, the James Bond series offers a particularly effective distillation of the elements of action violence that audiences seem to crave most, even as that formula has shifted and adapted over the years in response to varying audience desires and generic change in other action films.

James Bond is, like all action heroes, an essentially violent character, which is emphasised repeatedly in references to his being 'licenced to kill'. This phrase is crucial to the character's appeal because, like the western hero, Bond's violence is legitimate – literally licenced by the British government as a force for global good. However, unlike the western hero, Bond's violence is not always restrained and not always in response to violence inflicted on him. Rather, as James Chapman (2000) points out, the James Bond series is, like Hitchcock's *Secret Agent* (1936), rare in its emphasis on the secret agent as assassin. This is particularly notable in the series' first entry *Dr. No* (1962), which introduces Bond (then played by Sean Connery) as a ruthless, cold and exacting secret agent who at one point guns down an unarmed man in cold blood. Bond's violence is not 'disciplined and pure' like that of the western hero, who never kills with his fists or by stabbing with a blade (Cawelti 1984: 88). Rather, Bond will kill with any means necessary, evinced in his second outing *From Russia With Love* (1963), which features a brutal, protracted hand-to-hand fight with an assassin (played by Robert Shaw) that ends with Bond stabbing him in the side and then strangling him with his own garrote.

Thus, Bond's sophisticated veneer, which would become more pronounced with subsequent films in the series, is really just a thin façade for a brutal instrument, a point that comes full circle with *Casino Royale* (2006) and its follow-up *Quantum of Solace* (2008), which serve as a self-conscious origin story to reinvigorate the increasingly silly series. *Casino Royale* opens with Bond (now played by Daniel Craig) carrying out his first two government-sanctioned killings, one of which is a ferocious fight in a bathroom in which Bond first attempts to drown his opponent in a sink before shooting him after he suddenly rises again. As a whole, the film brings a new level of verisimilitude to the series' violence and also returns it to a more morally ambiguous arena. When Bond bleeds, it looks like it hurts; when he returns to a poker game after a fistfight, we can see bruises and scrapes on his knuckles; and when he is viciously tortured, his howls of pain make it feel real even as his refusal to divulge information reminds us of his ultimate power and control, making him an ideal figure of male identification and female desire.

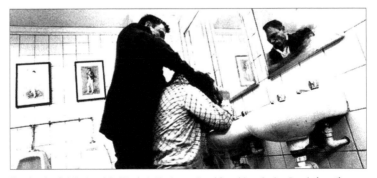

New levels of violent verisimilitude in the James Bond franchise: *Casino Royale* (2006)

While relatively new to the James Bond films, the torturing and maim-ing of the action hero is a fundamental component of the action genre and crucial to its meaning. As Rikke Schubart (2001) notes, there has been a substantial shift in the action film in the past twenty years away from pas-sion (elements of the film related to plot, myth, psychology and emotion) and towards acceleration (elements of spectacle, affect and exhilaration). As a whole, the Bond series has moved steadily in the direction of accel-eration, with each film expanding in terms of the scope and regularity of the action sequences. *Casino Royale*, however, returns elements of pas-sion to the character of James Bond, presenting him as a suffering martyr who ends the film standing above a wounded villain with machine gun in hand, a potent symbol of his righteous power. Thus, the James Bond of *Casino Royale* has more in common with earlier action heroes like Sylvester Stallone's John Rambo in *First Blood* (1982) and Mel Gibson's Martin Riggs in *Lethal Weapon*, characters who suffer before their vengeance/resurrec-tion, whose 'heroism is born out of loss and crisis' (Schubart 2001: 194). The majority of modern action heroes embody what Don Simpson and Jerry Bruckheimer, the producers behind *Beverly Hills Cop*, *Top Gun* and *Bad Boys* call 'the emotion of triumph' (Taylor 1989: 143), which relishes vic-tory for its own sake and has no room for moral uncertainty, masochistic suffering or emotional vulnerability. In these narratives violence is a tool for action heroes to prove their superiority; thus, unlike the traditional western, which uses moral codes to justify its violence, in modern action movies the end – victory at all costs – justifies the means, which invites the (presumably male) audience to indulge in narcissistic identification and pleasure.

Film violence is usually least enjoyable when it is taken seriously, which is why the action film has developed a sophisticated means of infusing its violence with humour, thereby ensuring the audience that their enjoyment of screen bloodshed is acceptable because it's all in good fun. This form of mixing comedy and graphic violence is particularly notable in action films of the 1990s, which employ this balance as a legitimating framework to make violence 'palatable for both audiences and regulatory authorities' (King 2004: 129).

One of the most effective means of using humour as a distanc-ing device to make violence more pleasurable is the witty quip, pun or one-liner, which acts as a release valve following a violent episode. Eric

Lichtenfeld notes that, while the use of the one-liner had its 'golden age' in the 1980s in action movies starring Arnold Schwarzenegger, Chuck Norris, Sylvester Stallone and Clint Eastwood, it has cinematic roots that date back several decades. He notes John Wayne growling 'That'll be the day' in *The Searchers*, which was so effective that Buddy Holly turned it into a song the next year. However, it is arguably the James Bond films that solidified the use of one-liners and puns to offset the potentially displeasurable effects of film violence. Tony Bennett and Janet Woollacott note how Bond's responses to his own use of violence in the films were significantly altered from Ian Fleming's source novels. In comparing *Goldfinger* with its literary source, they note that, after Bond electrocutes a villain in a bathtub, the killing 'is followed not by cynical and bitter reflection but by the one line joke, "Shocking, positively shocking"' (1987: 152). Like any generic component, Bond uttering an amusing quip after dispatching a villain became an expected part of the formula and functioned as a kind of wink to the audience, again assuring them that there was no need to take any of this too seriously.

In addition to humour, we can see the pleasure in action violence embodied in the shift from physical to technological violence, which, like the quip, functions to distance the audience from the discomfort associated with viewing cinematic bloodshed. Thomas Leitch shows that modern action films have shifted the locus of action from the performative male body to various technologies, specifically guns. We have already noted the western's embrace of larger and more powerful weapons in the 1950s, but this impulse can be seen as early as Howard Hawks's *The Dawn Patrol* (1930), which emphasises the pilots' control over their planes, and *The Adventures of Robin Hood*, which shows the victory of expert archers over expert swordsmen. The James Bond series is particularly emphatic about the role of technology, and we can see the shift between *Dr. No*, in which Bond is notably physical and relies almost entirely on his wits and his body to survive, and *From Russia With Love*, in which he is first outfitted with various 'gadgets' that conveniently come into play and save his life later in the film. In this film, it is a briefcase that contains a knife and an explosive charge of lethal gas. In later films the gadgets become more and more technologically sophisticated, even as their ultimate goal – the death of an enemy – remains constant. As we saw earlier, *From Russia With Love* also featured a protracted fistfight to the death, a scenario that would become more and more rare in succeeding films. This is also true of the majority of action films, which distance the hero from the death he inflicts by making guns the primary means of violence. Despite the seemingly limitless potential for firepower that cinematic weaponry represents, it works in conjunction with the legitimising narrative to make the hero's violence that much more palatable because, to return to the western, it suggests a level of proficiency and purity that both ennobles and sanitises the violence.

4 CASE STUDY: VIOLENCE AND THE NEW AMERICAN CINEMA

> The killing, connived at in the darkness, is the secret horror, and it surfaces in one bloody outburst after another. It surfaces so often that after a while it doesn't surprise us, and the recognition that the killing is an integral part of the business policy takes us a long way from the fantasy outlaws of old movies.
>
> Pauline Kael (1994: 435), from her review of *The Godfather*

At this point, we have looked at film violence from a number of angles, considering issues of definition, its historical development across world cinema and how it is used in and shapes the ideology of some of the most popular film genres. It should be clear that film violence is not a simple category or thing, as it is often made out to be. As a concept and filmmaking practice, violence needs to be interrogated on multiple fronts – historically, aesthetically, ideologically – before any kinds of conclusions can be drawn. Violence has been with the cinema since its inception, and if recent box-office trends are any indication, it has only grown in popularity and will continue to be with us for the foreseeable future.[1] Filmmakers both innovative and exploitative have made film violence the core of their work, and the multifaceted results are testament to how flexible and meaningful violence on the silver screen can be.

To conclude, we will examine one particular case study at length as an example of how engaging with and questioning film violence from a variety of perspectives can help us to better understand its role in the cinema. While there is an ocean of possibilities for such a case study, we will focus on the New American Cinema of the late 1960s and 1970s. There are several reasons for this. First, this particular era of filmmaking is especially notable for its violence. As we saw briefly in chapter two, this was the period immediately following the replacement of the Production Code with the MPAA ratings system, which allowed a new freedom in depicting violence in Hollywood films. Secondly, the young filmmakers who were coming to the fore of the American cinema at this time – Francis Ford Coppola, William Friedkin, Martin Scorsese, Steven Spielberg, Brian De Palma, to name a few – were particularly eager and willing to explore representations of violence in their films for various reasons, which range from responding to the uneasy zeitgeist of the 1960s, to aesthetic experimentation. Therefore, this case study will explore the notable prevalence of violence in the New American Cinema by examining its relationship to cultural and institutional changes, as well as individual filmmakers of merit. It will conclude with a brief examination of the 1970s films of Francis Ford Coppola, which in many ways encapsulate how violence was being deployed by this new generation of filmmakers.

Cultural and institutional changes

To fully understand how film violence is depicted in any one film, much less a number of films that can be said to comprise a 'movement' or 'era', we have to consider the cultural and industrial practices that helped to shape it. The late 1960s and early 1970s was a fervid period of experimentation in film violence largely because there was a series of important changes, both in how the major Hollywood studios operated and in the American culture. There are three factors during this time that are particularly relevant for understanding how violence was represented in the films of the New American Cinema: the dissolution of the Production Code and the creation of the ratings system; the cultural climate change resulting from the Vietnam War, the Civil Rights movement and increasing public violence; and the rising youth audience.

As we saw in chapter two, starting in the mid-1930s the Production Code was the single most important factor determining how violence was depicted in American cinema. However, by the early 1950s, the Code was being criticised more and more for being antiquated and useless, and it was being challenged with increasing frequency by filmmakers with artistic and economic clout, including Otto Preminger (*The Moon is Blue*, 1953; *The Man With the Golden Arm*, 1956) and Elia Kazan (*Baby Doll*, 1956), as well as foreign directors like Michelangelo Antonioni, whose *Blow-up* (1966), was distributed in the US by Metro-Goldwyn-Mayer, a member studio of the MPAA, under a separate, non-MPAA subsidiary when it was denied a Production Code Seal of Approval (see Lewis 2000: 146–8). In response to the Code's inability to serve the industry's needs, the MPAA created an age-based, exhibitor-enforced ratings system that was officially put into effect on 1 November 1968. Under the guise of preserving artistic freedom for filmmakers, this system codified into a set of guidelines the idea that different films are appropriate or inappropriate for different audiences based on their age.[2] Filmmakers responded almost immediately, expanding and elaborating on the kinds of violence audiences in the mid-1960s had seen in films like *Bonnie and Clyde*, *The Dirty Dozen* (1967), *In Cold Blood* (1967), *Point Blank* (1967) and *Bullitt* (1968). In the five years following the creation of the ratings system, filmmakers young and old worked with Hollywood studios to produce numerous films with intense levels of graphic violence that would have been unthinkable only five years earlier: *The Wild Bunch*, *Soldier Blue*, *Catch-22* (1970), *Dirty Harry*, *The French Connection*, *The Godfather* (1972) and *The Exorcist*, to name but a few.

Indirectly, but just as important to the rise of graphic violence at this time, was the changing social climate in America. As Tom Shachtman notes, during the 1960s, 'With each passing year the times themselves seemed to become more violent' (1983: 52), evidenced by more than a dozen Civil Rights leaders being assassinated between 1965 and 1968; gun homicides increasing by 15–20 per cent each year; and the rate of all violent crime doubling. Audiences were also faced with the violence of the war in Vietnam in newspapers, magazines and, most importantly, on television, and some filmmakers, especially Sam Peckinpah and Arthur Penn, saw the blood-soaked newscasts as an imperative to make film violence more realistic (see Prince 1998). They felt that they could no longer treat death and violence with restraint because much of the American public was, for the first time, fully aware of what it looked like when bullets and shrapnel damaged the human body. Peckinpah claimed that he used graphic violence in his films to make a point about violence itself: 'I use violence as it *is*. It's ugly, brutalising, and bloody fucking awful. It's not fun and games … it's a terrible, ugly thing' (quoted in Farber 1969: 8; emphasis in original). Similarly, Arthur Penn contended:

America is a country of people who act out their views in violent ways. Let's face it: Kennedy was shot. We're in Vietnam shooting people and getting shot ... It is the American society, and I would have to personify it by saying that it is a violent one. So why not make films about it. (Quoted in Bouzereau 1996: 11)

The violence of the times literally found its way into several films, including Haskell Wexler's *Medium Cool* (1968), whose cynical portrait of the American media was underscored by actual footage of the riots outside the Democratic national convention in Chicago, and the documentary *Gimme Shelter* (1970), which gained instant notoriety because it climaxes with the stabbing of an 18-year-old black man named Meredith Hunter by a member of the Hell's Angels at the Rolling Stones' legendary Altamont concert. Although the camera captured only the first fleeting seconds of Hunter's murder, the moment is replayed twice in the film as Mick Jagger watches it on the editing machine and co-director David Maysles slows down the scene so Jagger (and the audience) can see exactly what happens.

These increasingly violent films found their most willing viewers in a new audience comprised largely of teenagers, college students and young adults that had emerged as a powerful market force in the 1950s and 1960s (see Doherty 1988). By 1968, 48 per cent of box-office admissions went to 16–24-year-olds, and 54 per cent of that group were 'frequent moviegoers' (see Doherty 1988: 231). Not surprisingly, this audience, which was also better educated and more affluent than previous Hollywood audiences, had different tastes and tolerances than the older moviegoing demographic, which meant that they were more interested in seeing edgier fare like horror films, spaghetti westerns and exploitation cheapies – all of which had gained prominence during the decline of the Production Code. As J. Hoberman and Jonathan Rosenbaum put it, this audience had 'a demand for a new kind of product which was largely defined by its *devaluation* in relation to the respectable and cultured adult mind' (1983: 115; emphasis in original), which frequently involved representations of violence. After a while, young moviegoers became 'experts' in conventions of film violence, leading John Fraser to note that 'the young may in some ways be more accurate than some of their elders in their perceptions of a good deal of fictional violence, and better able to distinguish between realistic and stylised violences, intentionally and unintentionally comic ones, and so on, than is often allowed for' (1974: 8–9). This also meant that such viewers were more willing and eager to shift between high and low genres. They could readily appreciate the differences between the stark, symbolic and psychological violence in European art films by Michaelangelo Antonioni and Ingmar Bergman and the graphic physical violence of B-grade thrillers and horror movies. Thus, as Robert Kolker notes, following the graphically violent films of the late 1960s, 'aesthetics, prosthetics, cinematic ritual, and cultural consent sutured violence into the very structure of cinema' (2000: 50). Thus, while violence has been a part of the structure of cinema since its very inception, starting in the 1970s audiences were more aware of it because it was more direct, open and graphic than it had ever been before.

The film school generation

This era also witnessed the emergence of a new generation of American filmmakers who cut their own path through Hollywood, reimagining what constituted mainstream filmmaking practices and temporarily turning the system on its head. These filmmakers were markedly different from their forebears of the classical Hollywood era (1920s–1950s) in that they had been raised on television and were among the first to study film in recently created university graduate programmes and professional schools, rather than entering the industry and working their way through an apprentice system. This so-called 'Film School Generation' was something unique in the history of American cinema: its constituents were fully conversant in the history of film and deeply revered such masters as Orson Welles, Alfred Hitchcock and Howard Hawks, yet they were also fully in tune with the emerging youth market and understood that Hollywood cinema needed to be reworked if it was to maintain its relevance. They were also well versed in recent European cinema, and one of their hallmarks was the melding of art film aesthetics with traditional Hollywood genres, which resulted in an alchemic transformation of violence in American movies.

While these young filmmakers were highly educated and had strong artistic sensibilities, it is arguable that they never would have made it to the fore of American cinema if the Hollywood studios had not been struggling through a major recession. With collective losses of $300 to $400 million from 1969 to 1971 and a dwindling audience that had shrunk to a historic low of 15.8 million per week in 1971 (see Cook 2000: 9–14), many Hollywood studios were on the brink of collapse. Although the film industry had met the challenges posed by television and the expanding world of leisure activities in the 1950s, it had become mired in behind-the-curve thinking by the mid-1960s, feebly attempting to capitalise on the huge success of *The Sound of Music* (1965) with a series of expensive musicals that flopped one after the other (see Schatz 1992: 14). For the first time in their history, the Hollywood studios were being taken over by larger, widely diversified corporations. While this essentially saved the studios from bankruptcy and gave them immediate injections of much-needed cash, it also meant they were reduced from being independent, autonomous companies to divisions of much larger entities that were run by CEOs who had no experience with the movie business.

Thus, due to a combination of studio desperation to find 'the next big thing' and their new parent companies' general ignorance about how the system worked, a space was opened for young, relatively inexperienced filmmakers to make major commercial films their own way. As Peter Lev puts it, 'The 1970s were the true era of "Nobody knows anything", a period of uncertainty and disarray in the Hollywood film industry' (2000: xvi).

Auteurist violence

The changes in the film industry and the general cultural climate in the late 1960s – massive ruptures that resulted in significant changes in Hollywood production practices, ideologies, audience composition and film aesthetics – helped to create an atmosphere particularly conducive to the exploration of film violence within mainstream Hollywood.

Hollywood's financial uncertainty and artistic disarray helped open doors for the filmmakers of the Film School Generation, who produced a relatively short-lived, but deeply influential renaissance of American film built largely on film violence. As Robert Kolker has noted, the New American Cinema is best understood as a temporary intervention in the dominant mode of Hollywood film practices, both aesthetically and industrially. It provided 'brief freedom ... to be alone within a structure that momentarily entertained some experimentation' (2000: 9).

Despite being short-lived, the New American Cinema was profoundly influential, especially in depicting violence. While there are many characteristics that bind together the young directors who first made their mark in this era, what virtually all of them have in common is the reworking of film violence visually, narratively and thematically. With only a few exceptions, every filmmaker associated with the New American Cinema experimented with representations of violence. They brought it front and centre in their films, drawing the viewer's attention to the long-standing role violence had played in Hollywood cinema while simultaneously making it something new and even radical. Part of this was the brashness with which these filmmakers used violence, enhancing its thematic impact with new levels of visual realism that had rarely if ever been witnessed by mainstream audiences. They brought a new way of seeing violence to the cinema – a new sensibility – although their innovations would ultimately be subsumed into the dominant practices of the Hollywood industry.

Early on critics and audiences recognised the filmmakers of the New American Cinema as auteurs, both individually and as a collective. Central to the idea of the auteur is his or her ability to reshape well-worn and familiar conventions, which is arguably what drew so many New American filmmakers to violent themes. As violence has always been central to the cinema, particularly American cinema, it makes sense that filmmakers eager to distinguish themselves would gravitate towards it as a means to leave their mark, especially since it was also proving popular at the box office. The implementation of the ratings system in 1968 had given them room to explore violence visually and thematically in ways that had not been available to filmmakers of the previous generation. Film violence gave them something to which they could add harder edges and wield with a new authority that marked them as something innovative and decidedly 'in the moment'. They were among the first filmmakers to combine graphic violence with thematic complexity, proving that visceral onscreen bloodshed could be used seriously, not just for exploitation. As a cornerstone of the New American Cinema, film violence was a concrete means by which these young, largely untested filmmakers could build on what their predecessors had done, but also distinguish themselves as new and powerful.

While the term 'New American Cinema' is fairly broad in regards to what it encompasses, it is generally understood as including those filmmakers who first made their mark in the American cinema in the late 1960s and early 1970s. Many of them were among the first to graduate from professional and university film schools (for example, Francis Ford Coppola, George Lucas, Martin Scorsese, Paul Schrader), while others never attended film school at all (Steven Spielberg got his start as an intern at Universal Studios; Brian De Palma studied theatre at Sarah Lawrence College). It also includes some older filmmakers who were already established by the mid-1960s (for example, Arthur Penn, Sam Peckinpah, Robert Altman, Woody Allen, Stanley Kubrick), as well as a few Europeans who migrated to Hollywood (such as Milos Forman, Roman Polanski, John Boorman). However broadly or narrowly we wish to constitute this particular category, it is still inescapable that the vast majority of filmmakers included were either known primarily for making violent films or had experimented in some way with film violence either before or after they had secured some renown. As a result, most of the landmark films of this era are notably violent in form and content. Before looking at some of the filmmakers who were particularly well known for their violent films, it will be instructive to look at those who are not in order to illustrate just how pervasive was the desire of this generation of filmmakers to explore film violence, even if it was not necessarily their *métier*.

We can start with Peter Bogdanovich, who was a film programmer and critic who had befriended a number of luminaries of the classical era, most notably Orson Welles, before becoming a film director. His best known films are self-conscious throwbacks to the classical era of American cinema with which he was so enraptured: the small-town melodrama of *The Last Picture Show* (1971), the screwball antics of *What's Up, Doc?* (1972), the Depression-era odd-couple comedy of *Paper Moon* (1973). His tendencies in filmmaking lean towards the comic and the touching, yet his debut film was *Targets* (1968), an unnerving portrait of a seemingly normal young man who has a psychic breakdown and goes on a killing spree that was purposefully reminiscent of Charles Whitman's deadly attack at the University of Texas at Austin only two years earlier. The film was made at the behest of low-budget producer Roger Corman, who gave Bogdanovich less than a month and $125,000 to make the feature and required that he incorporate footage from a 1963 Corman-produced film called *The Terror* and use screen veteran Boris Karloff, who contractually owed Corman two more days of work.

Thematically, *Targets* cuts to the heart of real-life social violence in the US, which, in 1968, was at the peak of inner-city riots, homicides and political assassinations. The film is fraught with the tension of impending violence in even the most banal people, but without displacing its anxiety onto the past as had been done in *Bonnie and Clyde* and *The Wild Bunch*. The film also deals explicitly with its own genre by noting the shift horror had undergone in the 1960s, moving away from inhuman monsters residing in distant, exotic lands (Dracula in Transylvania, for example) and towards a recognition of horror as 'both American and familial' (Wood 1996: 185). Boris Karloff (best known for defining the role of Frankenstein's monster in the 1930s Universal series) plays Byron Orlock, an ageing horror movie veteran who decides to retire because, as he argues, he is identified too much with a kind of horror that no longer scares people – the kind that takes place in old, gothic castles in remote lands. Thus, *Targets* both depicts and reflects upon the kinds of violence that people genuinely feared at the time and its relationship to the cinema.

Another significant figure of the New American Cinema not often discussed in terms of violence is Robert Altman, who was already an established, if not particularly well-known, director by the mid-1960s, with a handful of features and dozens of television show episodes under his belt. Altman is usually discussed in terms of his decentralising narrative structures, which tend to include multiple protagonists and interweaving storylines, as well as his sometimes radically revisionist takes on traditional genre material (the western in *McCabe & Mrs. Miller*, film noir in *The Long Goodbye* (1973), the musical in *Nashville* (1975)). Yet, many of his films hinge on violence, to the point that there is a consistent pattern in its representation: 'acts of violence continually break out in Altman's films … always there to punctuate the tenuous calm of any given scene and indicate the disruption and potential violence that underlie any situation' (Kolker 2000: 347).

Altman's breakthrough film *M*A*S*H* (1970) was a radical mixing of anarchic comedy and grisly war violence. Set in a mobile surgical hospital near the frontlines during Korea (a thinly disguised stand-in for Vietnam), the film features numerous scenes in which the comical Army surgeons try to plug squirting arteries and otherwise mend war-torn bodies, all of which is depicted with a flat, convincing realism that contrasts with the silliness of the comedy. As with the mixing of tones we saw in the horror film, Altman's juxtaposition of laughs and bloody viscera is inherently transgressive, and we can see violence as a fundamental element of his larger aesthetic impulse to break apart conventional Hollywood narrative and challenge the ideological status quo. His work represents a key example of how an innovative director might use film violence not to exploit for shock value, but as one functional component of a larger artistic and thematic vision.

Similarly, Mike Nichols is usually not associated with violent films. Coming from a background in improvisational performance and directing Broadway theatre, he broke into American film with his controversial drama *Who's Afraid of Virginia Woolf?* (1966), whose coarse language and harsh themes made it one of the key films that led the MPAA to discard the Production Code in favour of a ratings system. His follow-up was *The Graduate* (1967), a generation-gap comedy inflected with European art film stylistics that became the top-grossing film of the 1960s and won Nichols an Academy Award for Best Director. Along with *Bonnie and Clyde* and *Cool Hand Luke* (1967), *The Graduate* was a seminal film of its era, centring around a marginalised antihero with whom the youth audience could identify. However, unlike *Bonnie and Clyde* and *Cool Hand Luke*, both of which rely on the tragic, violent deaths of their antiheroic protagonists, *The Graduate* focuses on interpersonal, rather than physical conflict (although the film does culminate with a purposefully absurd fight in which Dustin Hoffman's Benjamin Braddock fends off an entire wedding party with a large cross).

Given *The Graduate*'s success, there was much anticipation surrounding Nichols' follow-up project, an adaptation of Joseph Heller's 1961 absurdist World War Two novel *Catch-22*. The film was a commercial and critical failure when it was released in 1970, partially because its thunder had been stolen by the thematically similar but more approachable *M*A*S*H*. This partially accounts for why *Catch-22* is frequently ignored when discussing Nichols' career, but it may also be because it represents such a divergence from the kinds of films for which he is best known. However, this is precisely why it is such an important film, as it represents a conscious effort on the part of a New American auteur to explore film violence in challenging and provocative ways. As Robert Merrill and John L. Simons note, *Catch-22* 'succeeds when it develops visually a basic metaphor from Heller's book: the nightmarish and omnipresent danger of death in war. Nichols' film does not so much reprise the novel's truculent satire on American capitalism as tell a story about the traumatising fear of death, a fear that confuses the brain and blunts the conscience' (1994: 17). In making *Catch-22* his own, Nichols approached the material through the lens of violent death, which is decidedly 'omnipresent' throughout the film. Starting with the opening scene in which Captain Yossarian (Alan Arkin) is stabbed in the back by a mysterious assailant, the film is replete with scenes of violence that, while variously absurd and heartbreaking, are predominantly grim. The breadth of violent dark comedy is astounding, everything from characters talking blithely about profit margins while a plane crash-lands and burns in the background, to a notorious scene in which a character named Hungry Joe (Seth Allen) is unexpectedly sawed in half by a low-flying plane's propeller. The most shocking depiction of violence, however, and the one that draws powerful attention to the destruction of the human body by war, is a dreamlike sequence that is replayed in fragmented form five times throughout the film. It involves Yossarian attempting to comfort a young gunner who has been wounded during a bomb raid. In each successive version of the scene, we learn a little bit more about what has happened. At first, we think only his leg is wounded, but then we learn that he has some kind of significant abdominal injury which is horrifically verified in the final sequence when Yossarian pulls up his shirt and we see the gunner's exposed intestines and other internal organs ooze out. Although only onscreen for a few seconds, it is a truly shocking moment that burns an imprint in the mind's eye, and its message about the inherent materiality of the human body – that, in the end, we are all just meat – underscores the film's obsession with the violence of death and dying.

A truly shocking revelation that underscores the obsession with death and dying common to many films of the New American Cinema: *Catch-22* (1970)

As the examples of Peter Bogdanovich, Robert Altman and Mike Nichols demonstrate, violence was an important component of their development as New American Cinema auteurs. Even if it was not central to their cinematic identity, film violence was still prevalent to the point that they felt the need to experiment with it on some level, and their success or failure with it helped to shape their subsequent reputations. At the same time, for many of the most visible and well-regarded filmmakers of the New American Cinema, their reputations were shaped almost entirely around representations of violence, at least in their early films.

Despite making films as varied as the feminist melodrama *Alice Doesn't Live Here Anymore* (1974) and the big-band musical *New York, New York* (1977), Martin Scorsese is best known for his most violent films, including *Mean Streets* (1973), an intimate character study of low-level hoods in New York's Little Italy; *Taxi Driver*, a brooding exploration of an unhinged Vietnam veteran's personal war against the moral decay of modern society; and *Raging Bull*, a powerfully disturbing portrait of real-life boxer Jake La Motta's inability to contain his violence in the ring. During this same time Brian De Palma staked his place in American cinema by consciously following in the footsteps of Alfred Hitchcock with a series of stylish thrillers that were heavy on violence and were frequently accused of being misogynistic. Although he started by making low-budget comedies, De Palma made a name for himself with the overtly Hitchcockian thriller *Sisters* (1973), which was as obsessed with voyeurism as it was with complex tracking shots. De Palma's other 1970s films include *Carrie* (1976), an adaptation of Stephen King's first novel about a picked-on adolescent girl with telekinetic powers; *Obsession* (1976), a reworking of Hitchcock's *Vertigo* (1958) that, while featuring significantly less physical violence than De Palma's other films of the period, is heavy with penetrating psychological violence (the screenplay was by Paul Schrader, who also wrote *Taxi Driver*); *The Fury* (1978), another story about a girl with telekinesis that is notable for its concluding image of John Cassavettes' entire body exploding, which De Palma draws out by showing it multiple times from multiple angles in slow-motion; and *Dressed to Kill*, a reworking of *Psycho* that raised the ire of feminists and led to numerous public protests.

As a concentrated example, we will conclude by looking at the films produced by Francis Ford Coppola, arguably the most successful and powerful New American auteur during the 1970s. Considered 'the guiding light' of the

Film School Generation by many of his peers, Coppola was 'the vanguard figure of this new breed of directors' (Cook 1998: 14–15). He was the first of the young New American Cinema filmmakers to make a significant splash in the industry, although it took him nearly a decade to do so. Coppola's first film as director was a low-budget, black-and-white 'axploitation' film called *Dementia 13* (1963), which he shot for producer Roger Corman after convincing him that he could make an entire film using standing sets, insert photography and cast and crew from another Corman production that was about to wrap in Ireland. *Dementia 13* is a grisly little thriller, one of the many *Psycho*-knock-offs that glutted the US and British markets in the early 1960s. The film features several scenes in which characters are murdered with an axe, including a very brief, but graphic decapitation that was actually shot by Jack Hill, another of Corman's protégés, when Corman worried that the film was not violent enough. Coppola's next three films – *You're a Big Boy Now* (1966), *Finian's Rainbow* (1968) and *The Rain People* (1969) – were all nonviolent affairs that garnered little critical attention and even less at the box office, but during the 1970s Coppola built a towering reputation as a powerful and commanding artistic visionary with a quartet of violent films that simultaneously tapped into the deep roots of the mythic and struck the zeitgeist's nerves of paranoia and unease.

Coppola's first big success was *The Godfather*, an epic, some might say Shakespearean, portrait of a mafia family that not only made the 32-year-old Coppola's career, but also helped to pull the troubled Hollywood industry out of the economic doldrums in which it had been mired since the late 1960s. Based on the pulpy bestseller published in 1969 by Mario Puzo, *The Godfather* is a deeply violent film, not only in terms of the actions it represents (multiple assassinations, vicious beatings and the infamous terrorising of an egomaniacal Hollywood producer with a decapitated horse's head), but in the underlying thematic focus on the shifting nature of power and its corrupting influence. As Jake Horsley puts it, 'the strange and terrible grandeur which [the film's violence] assumes is due to the fact that the violence is not simply performed – it is *ordained*' (1999a: 120; emphasis in original).

The film tells the story of the fictional Corleone family and how the family's power moves from the ageing father, Don Vito Corleone (Marlon Brando), to his youngest son, Michael (Al Pacino). Power is seen as the ultimate commodity, more important than money or possessions, which, like the classic gangster films of the 1930s, turns *The Godfather* into a twisted and tragic image of American enterprise. At the beginning of the film, Michael, a hero of World War Two who has gone out of his way to separate himself, is staunchly against taking part in the family's illegal businesses. But, as the film progresses, it becomes increasingly clear that he is only deluding himself, and his evolution into a cold-hearted, ruthless leader, much more dangerous than his father ever was, is central to the film's violent undertones. Overt violence frequently explodes onto the surface, never so memorably as in the montage sequence – the very epitome of the film's *ordained* violence – that cuts together reverent scenes of Michael acting as godfather to his sister's child with the brutal violence of his henchmen murdering the family's enemies. The two opposing halves of the sequence show Michael's dual nature: in the legitimate sense, he is becoming godfather to a child, a highly respected and religious position. But, in a larger sense, by ordering the murder of all his enemies, he confirms his position as head of the Corleone family – the new Godfather.

Coppola followed with *The Godfather Part II* (1974), which is more thematically and structurally complex than its predecessor in telling two stories at once. One half of the movie deals with Vito Corleone (Robert De Niro) as a young man, explaining how he came to America at age nine after his father, brother and mother were murdered by the local mafia boss in Sicily. There, among the immigrants and tenements of New York's Little Italy, he slowly rises to power and prominence. The other half of the film follows Michael Corleone after he has assumed power of the family in the 1950s, sold off all their interests in New York and concentrated on the gambling and hotel prospects in Las Vegas. By this point, his metamorphosis is complete, and he is even more ruthless and dangerous than he was at the end of the first film, exemplified in his willingness to order the murder of his own brother, Fredo (John Cazale). While *The Godfather* was criticised in some circles for romanticising the mafia, *The Godfather Part II* takes a different approach by focusing on the deterioration of the Corleone family; whereas the first film had rooted the family's success in its solidarity and loyalty as a family, the sequel shows how it begins to unravel at the seams once that solidarity and loyalty begin to falter, replaced instead with divorce, abortion and eventually fratricide. In juxtaposing Michael's slow descent during the late 1950s with Vito's slow ascent during the mid-1920s, the film highlights the role of violence in both attaining and losing power, suggesting quite powerfully the truth of the old aphorism that those who live by the sword shall die by it.

The same year that *The Godfather Part II* was released also saw the release of *The Conversation*, a tragic thriller about electronic surveillance that tapped directly into post-Watergate fears of spying, political corruption and unchecked power. Coppola creates a strikingly closed sense of claustrophobia and suspicion, digging into our primal fear that we can never be alone, that someone is always watching. The film's protagonist, Harry Caul (Gene Hackman), is a surveillance expert – 'the best bugger on the West Coast', as one of his chief rivals puts it. When the film opens, Caul and his assistant, Stan (John Cazale), are in the middle of a difficult assignment: a mysterious man known only as The Director has paid Caul to record a conversation between his wife (Cindy Williams) and another man (Frederic Forrest) as they walk in circles in a park in the middle of downtown San Francisco during a crowded lunchtime period. Caul breaks his strict rule of not getting personally involved in his work when he realises that, when he turns the tape over to The Director, a murder may ensue. He does not know for sure, but several years earlier he was involved in another assignment that resulted in three deaths, and he does not want to live through it again.

Thus, although there is little conventional 'violent action' in *The Conversation*, every frame of the film is heavy with a sense of impending violence. Caul's paranoia is based on his experiences, which have taught him that surveillance is not a neutral act, but a form of violence against others' privacy that can lead to physical consequences. We can also look at the film as a slow build-up to violence, as all of Harry's fears seem to come true in the final moments when we obliquely witness a particularly brutal murder that is all the more disturbing for its ambiguity. When Harry breaks into the hotel room where he suspects the murder has taken place, he finds it completely devoid of any signs of struggle. However, when Harry flushes the bathroom toilet, he discovers that it has been stuffed with bloody towels, which causes the toilet to well up and spill blood and water onto the bathroom floor. Although the blood and towels are physical evidence confirming Harry's worst fears, Coppola stages the scene like a nightmare, investing it with a potent metaphorical weight that turns a gory, revolting image into a symbol of the darkest recesses of corruption and the abuse of power overflowing onto our collective feet.

The nightmare-like staging gives the vision of blood a potent metaphorical weight: *The Conversation* (1974)

Coppola finished the decade with his infamous Vietnam epic *Apocalypse Now*, a film of grandiose scale and thematic ambitions that portended the end of the New American Cinema (with Michael Cimino's disastrous *Heaven's Gate* finishing the job a year later), which was quickly losing ground to the post-*Star Wars* blockbuster mentality of making film violence increasingly cartoonish and impersonal and therefore easily palatable to the mass audience. *Apocalypse Now*, on the other hand, is an inspired vision of unbridled violence, even if that vision eventually sinks into a form of chaos that mimics the film's thematic concerns with insanity.

The film is based loosely on Joseph Conrad's 1902 novella *Heart of Darkness*, with which it shares thematic concerns about the tensions between civilisation and savagery and the metaphoric use of an upriver journey into the jungle to represent a descent into the darkness of human violence. Coppola and co-writer John Milius, who was also part of the Film School Generation, moved the narrative out of nineteenth-century Africa and into the quagmire of the Vietnam War in the early 1970s. The ultimate destination of the journey is somewhere in Cambodia, where a decorated Green Beret officer named Walter E. Kurtz (Marlon Brando) has apparently gone insane and marshalled an army of devoted followers. Because Kurtz is operating with 'unsound methods', the military sends Captain

Benjamin Willard (Martin Sheen) on a secret mission to 'terminate Kurtz's command'. In other words, Willard is being sent to assassinate one of his fellow officers.

Madness and violence are the film's organising principles, which makes *Apocalypse Now* as disjointed as it is powerfully unnerving. As a journey, the film's destination is a place of complete insanity, with Kurtz as a despot-philosopher ruling over a savage army deep in the primeval jungle. The final portion of the film at Kurtz's compound turns it explicitly into a horror movie (a literalisation of 'The horror! The horror!'), with corpses, severed limbs and disembodied heads scattered throughout the frame – constant reminders of death and desecration. Each step of Willard's journey up the river is a step deeper into this chaos. The irony, of course, is that his journey begins in the madness of the Vietnam War, which had an insanity all of its own. Willard's first contact is the deranged, gun-crazy Lieutenant Colonel Kilgore (Robert Duvall), who thinks little of destroying a Vietnamese village because the beaches around it have waves ideal for surfing. The question becomes, then, why is Kurtz insane by military standards but Kilgore not? Are the severed body parts adorning Kurtz's compound any worse than the bodies mutilated by Kilgore's aerial attack?

Apocalypse Now was received with a mixed response, although there was a fairly unanimous condemnation of the film's final scenes at Kurtz's compound, which were considered too dark, too rambling and too incoherent, much like Marlon Brando's much-maligned performance as Kurtz. Yet, this very ambiguity gives the film its greatest jolt for it clarifies the ultimate meaninglessness of Willard's journey. Kurtz could not have possibly lived up to Willard's expectations or ours because he is ultimately just a human being, even though he is raised to god-like status in the eyes of his deranged followers. That these final scenes are rambling and murky, filled with long-winded exposition and gaudy visual effects, is arguably the best way the film could end. It is, in fact, the very antithesis of the anticlimax many accused it of being because Willard truly finds the heart of darkness, and it is not that far removed from where he started. Of course, however one views the ending or the film as a whole, it should not detract from the fact that one of the most powerful and financially successful Hollywood directors would stake his reputation on such a risky and expensive project, one infused with uneasy violence that was difficult for audiences to comprehend and risked alienating them completely.

As we have seen, in all four of Coppola's films from the 1970s, violence in many forms – physical, emotional, psychological, legitimate and criminal (although the latter two are rarely clear-cut) – is the thematic backbone, and Coppola orchestrates this violence with a mixture of aesthetic approaches, which was a hallmark of the New American Cinema, from the *cinéma vérité*-inspired grit of William Friedkin's *The French Connection*, to the shockingly realistic maiming of bodies in Martin Scorsese's *Taxi Driver*, to the flamboyantly murderous glee of Brian De Palma's *Dressed to Kill*. For example, the 'Flight of the Valkyries' helicopter attack on a Vietnamese village in *Apocalypse Now* plays like a parody of an action movie sequence with its point-of-view shots from the nose of the attacking helicopters, the enormous explosions and the roaring Wagner music self-consciously played by Kilgore to frighten his intended targets. Coppola stages the sequence as an attention-grabbing stand-alone setpiece, and while we are meant to feel the rush of the excitement and danger, the underlying absurdity of the attack's purpose and the ambiguous nature of the enemy problematises the emotional responses other films have taught us to indulge without question. Similarly, the aforementioned montage in *The Godfather* in which Michael Corleone takes part in a religious ceremony while his thugs murder the family's enemies is staged as an operatic evocation of murderous hypocrisy, but it also hits on a gut level with its careful attention to the gory effects of dying in a hail of bullets (the most memorable is Moe Greene (Alex Rocco) being shot in the eye through his glasses while getting a massage).[3] There is also a similar effect in *The Conversation* when Harry witnesses a murder through the distorted glass wall separating his hotel balcony from the one next door. With only a single image – a blurred hand smearing blood against the glass – Coppola makes the violence physically palpable, but the scene resonates with psychological distress via his use of ragged, jump-cut editing borrowed from European art films and a shrieking synthesised musical score that sounds like it was drawn straight from a horror film. In mixing such seemingly disparate modalities to create a complex physical and psychological depiction of violence, Coppola embodies what was new and innovative and also shocking about the New American Cinema.

NOTES

chapter one

1 For a comprehensive overview of snuff films, mondo films and atrocity footage, see Kerkes and Slater (1994); see also Brottman (1995).

2 The physical effect that violent films can have on the audience is one reason why they are often viewed as 'low cinematic culture' and 'degraded cultural forms' (Hawkins 2000: 4–5; see also Williams 1995).

3 For example, in his review of the film on 1 January 1974, *Chicago Sun-Times* critic Roger Ebert wrote, '*The Texas Chain Saw Massacre* is as violent and gruesome and blood-soaked as the title promises – a real Grand Guignol of a movie.'

4 One exception is Martin Scorsese's *The Last Temptation of Christ* (1988), whose depiction of the crucifixion is more historically accurate than Mel Gibson's film, which draws heavily from Catholic iconography. However, many Christian viewers who saw Gibson's film were likely more familiar with sanitised images in films like *King of Kings* (1961) and *The Greatest Story Ever Told* (1965), which were then used as a point of comparison.

5 For a concise overview of the major research literature on the 'problem of the movies' from 1907–1940, see Jowett (1971).

6 For example, in 1948 the National Congress of Parents and Teachers set up a committee focused on wiping out objectionable media. Tellingly, Mrs L. W. Hughes, the group's associate president, mentioned movies, radio programmes and comic books, but held special attention for

the latter, arguing that, while all three media have 'abused the public trust', 'None have done so more grossly, however, than the publishers of comic books relying for their appeal on blood-thirsty violence' (Anon. 1948: 29).

7   According to Lawrence Alloway, the publication of Wertham's book was 'a peak of liberal hysteria' (1971: 65).

8   Dionysus was the Greek god of wine and of an orgiastic religion celebrating the power and fertility of nature. The ancient Greeks held yearly festivals to honour Dionysus, and many scholars believe that it was in these festivals that Greek tragedy originated. Interestingly, it was in his writings on Greek tragedy that Aristotle first elaborated a theory of catharsis through vicarious viewing of tragic events, which was later rearticulated and combined with the writings of Sigmund Freud to defend catharsis through viewing onscreen violence.

9   For an overview of the research literature on this topic, see Zillmann (1998).

10 See also the work of Steve Neale (1983) on screen masculinity.

chapter two

1   This scene was replayed in even more graphic fashion in the 1931 version starring Tallulah Bankhead.

2   It should be noted that there were multiple versions of the Production Code in circulation at different points in time. The specific listing of 'Repellent Subjects' at the end of the 'Particular Applications' was included on the typescript signed by the Board of Directors of the MPPDA on 31 March 1930 (see Maltby 1995: 51) and is also in the version of the Code printed as an appendix to Leonard J. Leff and Jerold L. Simmons' *The Dame in the Kimono* (1990). However, this section is left out entirely in the copy of the Code published in *Hollywood's Movie Commandments: A Handbook for Motion Picture Writers and Reviewers* (1937) by Olga J. Martin, who was the former secretary to PCA head Joseph Breen. Because of Martin's position, Thomas Doherty argues that this version of the Code can be considered 'the most complete, contemporaneous document consulted by Hollywood's in-house censors' (1999: 347).

3   The appeal of gangsters and criminality on the screen was also exploited in newsreels, including the two-part 1936 series *The March of Crime*, which used the guise of histrionic moralising about embellished true-crime stories as an excuse to show gory footage both recreated and real (including shots of beheaded Chinese criminals, and film footage of Elmer McGurdy's mummified body and John Dillinger's corpse in the morgue; see Schaefer 1999: 285).

4   This switch from the bad side to the good side was self-consciously used in the film's advertising. The ads proclaimed, 'PUBLIC ENEMY Becomes Soldier of the Law. Hollywood's Most Famous Bad Man Joins the *G Men* and Halts the March of Crime … The fact that Jimmy Cagney, the historic *Public Enemy* of 1931, now plays the lead in this epic of the end of gang-dom, makes its appeal inevitable!' (quoted in Leach 1975: 72).

5   Although not very reliable, it is interesting to note that Mirams compares his findings with the findings of Edgar Dale, who conducted one of the Payne Fund Studies on violence in US films in 1935. Mirams found that the US films of 1949–50 had exactly twice as many incidents of violence per film as Dale's survey of 15 years earlier. Mirams concludes that 'while the number of individual Hollywood films containing some crime and violence is not markedly greater now than two decades ago (88 per cent as compared with 84 per cent), the *intensity* of such manifestations is twice as marked' (1951: 5; emphasis in original).

6   *The Curse of Frankenstein*, which was distributed worldwide by Warner Bros., made $5 million on a budget of $160,000 (see McCarty 1984: 22).

7   When the British Film Institute restored *Dracula* in 2007, it required duplicate negatives of footage censored from the British version of the film that were only available in the vaults of Warner Bros., the film's US distributor (see Higgins & Ross 2007). One difference between the two versions is the aforementioned staking scene: in the British version, we do not see the stake actually driven in and blood come out. Also deleted are close-up shots of the vampire screaming and writhing in pain, which suggests that the unease of film violence was not just concerned with physical detail, but the representation of pain.

8   A scanned reproduction of the letter sent on 31 January 1961 by PCA head Geoffrey M. Shurlock to producer Richard Gordon is available as

part of the supplementary materials on the Criterion Collection's DVD of *Corridors of Blood*. While Shurlock notes that the film is acceptable 'in general' he notes the three scenes that must be cut due to their containing 'overly gory details'.

9   The confused state of *Eyes Without a Face* can be seen via its treatment during its initial theatrical release in the US in 1962, where it was edited, retitled *The Horror Chamber of Dr. Faustus*, and distributed as part of a double-bill with a cheap shocker called *The Manster*.

10 The connection between the shifting voyeuristic appeals of sex and violence is underscored by the fact that the first 'ghoulies' and 'roughies' were all directed by filmmakers who had originally started by making 'nudie' films: Lee Frost, Herschell Gordon Lewis, Doris Wishman and Russ Meyer.

11 *Blood Feast* was originally released with a gimmick in which white paper bags were given to audience members. The bags, half a million of which were reportedly distributed, advised viewers, 'You May Need This When You See *Blood Feast*' (see Curry 2000: 61).

12 In an initial review of *Night of the Living Dead* published in *Variety*, the critic wrote, 'The film casts serious aspersions on the integrity of its makers, distrib Walter Reade, the film industry as a whole and exhibs who book the pic, as well as raising doubts about the future of the regional cinema movement and the moral health of filmgoers who cheerfully opt for unrelieved sadism' (quoted in Hoberman and Rosenbaum 1983: 110).

13 Stephen Prince suggests this in his audio commentary on the Criterion Collection DVD edition of *The Naked Prey*.

14 Ironically, *Friday the 13th* (1980) was originally passed for theatrical distribution by the British Board of Film Classification (BBFC) uncut. According to BBFC Secretary James Ferman, it was because 'The murders were so far fetched, with knife blades coming up through beds into somebody, that it was clearly unreal … The nice thing about fantasy is all the time you can keep reminding yourself, "I can't get hurt, no one's going to get hurt, it's just make-believe".' Ferman then noted that, 'If you present it [violence] realistically, it impinges on your feelings, you haven't got that suspension of disbelief' (quoted in Mathews 1994: 228).

chapter three

1   In *The Movie Ratings Game*, Stephen Farber includes an interesting discussion about the difficulties *Soldier Blue* had making it through the MPAA ratings system without receiving an X rating for violence (see 1972: 67–9). Farber awarded the movie an R rating because he felt 'the brutality was used to make a valid social statement' (1972: 69), while another member of the board insisted that it would have to be passed as an X because 'the entire film was the most extreme portrait of human savagery and bestiality that she could imagine, and she sensed that a few snips would not mute the impact' (ibid.).

chapter four

1   In *Hollywood's Road to Riches* (2005), David Waterman compiled trends over a 35-year period (1967–2001) and found that Hollywood's output of what he calls 'violence-prone genres' (action, adventure, science fiction, thriller, horror, crime and war) rose from forty per cent in 1967 to seventy percent by 2001, with the production of action and adventure films both more than doubling.

2   The first declared objective of the new ratings system, according to an official brochure published by the MPAA in 1968, was 'To encourage artistic expression by expanding creative freedom' (quoted in Farber 1972: 112).

3   The image of Moe Greene being shot in the eye through his glasses is visually reminiscent of the climactic shock cut in the Odessa Steps sequence of *Battleship Potemkin* that depicts a woman being shot in a similar manner. In the annotated screenplay to *The Godfather*, Jenny M. Jones suggests that this might have been done on purpose: 'Moe Greene's particular mode of assassination in the film could also be an homage to the great Sergei Eisenstein's … *Battleship Potemkin* … Coppola has cited Eisenstein as the filmmaker who most influenced his decision to become a director' (2007: 222). Jones goes on to note that actor Alex Rocco reported that Coppola got the idea of the effect from 'a European film, and always wanted to do it', which could imply the Soviet-produced *Battleship Potemkin* (ibid.). In terms of the devel-

opment of violent representation, the images in the two films – separated by nearly five decades of cinema history and development – are intriguing in that Eisenstein created the effect of being shot via an edit, whereas Coppola had at his disposal special effects technologies designed by A. D. Flowers that could render the moment of violence in an unbroken take.

FILMOGRAPHY

The following filmography is not intended to be a comprehensive list of all the most violent or most important *violent* films ever made, but rather a concentrated sampling of films from the silent era to the present that have had an impact on depictions of violence in mainstream cinema and exemplify the film violence characteristic of their period.

300 (Zack Snyder, 2006, US)
A Bucket of Blood (Roger Corman, 1959, US)
A Clockwork Orange (Stanley Kubrick, 1971, UK)
A History of Violence (David Cronenberg, 2005, US/Germany)
All Quiet on the Western Front (Lewis Milestone, 1930, US)
Apocalypse Now (Francis Ford Coppola, 1979, US)
Armageddon (Michael Bay, 1998, US)
Bad Lieutenant (Abel Ferrara, 1992, US)
Baise-moi (Virginie Despentes, 2000, France)
Basic Instinct (Paul Verhoeven, 1992, US)
Bataan (Tay Garnett, 1943, US)
Batman (Tim Burton, 1989, US)
Batoru rowaiaru/Battle Royale (Kinji Fukasaku, 2000, Japan)
Beheading of a Chinese Prisoner (Sigmund Lubin, 1900, US)
Big Heat, The (Fritz Lang, 1953, US)
Birds, The (Alfred Hitchcock, 1963, US)
Birth of a Nation, The (D.W. Griffith, 1915, US)
Blackboard Jungle (Richard Brooks, 1955, US)
Blade Runner (Ridley Scott, 1982, US)
Blood Feast (Herschell Gordon Lewis, 1963, US)
Blue Velvet (David Lynch, 1986, US)
Bonnie and Clyde (Arthur Penn, 1967, US)
Bourne Ultimatum, The (Paul Greengrass, 2007, US)

Boyz N the Hood (John Singleton, 1991, US)

Braindead (aka *Dead-Alive*, Peter Jackson, 1992, New Zealand)

Bronenosets Potyomkin/Battleship Potemkin (Sergei Eisenstein, 1926, Soviet Union)

Brute Force (Jules Dassin, 1947, US)

Bullitt (Peter Yates, 1968, US)

Cannibal Holocaust (Ruggero Deodato, 1980, Italy)

Cape Fear (Martin Scorsese, 1991, US)

Catch-22 (Mike Nichols, 1970, US)

C'est arrivé près de chez vous/Man Bites Dog (Rémy Belvaux/André Bonzel/Benoît Poelvoorde, 1993, Belgium)

Cheat, The (Cecil B. DeMille, 1915, US)

Conversation, The (Francis Ford Coppola, 1974, US)

Cook, the Thief, His Wife, & Her Lover, The (Peter Greenaway, 1989, France/UK)

Corbett and Courtney Before the Kinetograph (Edison Company, 1894, US)

Corridors of Blood (Robert Day, 1959, UK)

Crash (David Cronenberg, 1996, Canada/UK)

Cuban Ambush (Edison Company, 1898, US)

Curse of Frankenstein, The (Terence Fisher, 1957, UK)

Das Cabinet des Dr. Caligari/The Cabinet of Dr. Caligari (Robert Wiene, 1919, Germany)

Davy Crockett, King of the Wild Frontier (Norman Foster, 1955, US)

Dawn of the Dead (George A. Romero, 1978, US)

Day of the Woman (aka *I Spit on Your Grave*, Meir Zarchi, 1978, US)

Death Wish (Michael Winner, 1974, US)

Deer Hunter, The (Michael Cimino, 1978, US)

Defilers, The (R. L. Frost, 1965, US)

Desperado (Robert Rodriguez, 1995, US)

Devil's Rejects, The (Rob Zombie, 2005, US)

Die Hard (John McTiernan, 1988, US)

Dip huet seung hung/The Killer (John Woo, 1989, Hong Kong)

Dirty Dozen, The (Robert Aldrich, 1967, US)

Dirty Harry (Don Siegel, 1971, US)

Django (Sergio Corbucci, 1966, Italy/Spain)

Do the Right Thing (Spike Lee, 1989, US)

Dr. Mabuse, der Spieler – Ein Bild der Zeit/Dr. Mabuse, the Gambler (Fritz Lang, 1922, Germany)

Dr. No (Terence Young, 1962, UK)
Dracula (Tod Browning, 1931, US)
Dracula (aka *Horror of Dracula*, Terence Fisher, 1958, UK)
Dressed to Kill (Brian De Palma, 1980, US)
Duel in the Sun (King Vidor, 1946, US)
Electrocuting an Elephant (Edison Company, 1903, US)
Evil Dead, The (Sam Raimi, 1982, US)
Execution of Czolgosz, With Panorama of Auburn Prison (Edwin S. Porter, 1901, US)
Execution of Mary, Queen of Scots, The (Edison Company, 1894, US)
Exorcist, The (William Friedkin, 1973, US)
Explosion of a Motor Car (Cecil M. Hepworth, 1900, US)
Fiend Without a Face (Arthur Crabtree, 1958, UK)
Fight Club (David Fincher, 1999, US)
Flesh for Frankenstein (Paul Morrissey, 1973, US/Italy/France)
Frankenstein (James Whale, 1931, US)
French Connection, The (William Friedkin, 1971, US)
Frenzy (Alfred Hitchcock, 1972, UK)
Friday the 13th (Sean S. Cunningham, 1980, US)
Funny Games (Michael Haneke, 1997, Austria)
Gekitotsu! Satsujin ken/The Street Fighter (Shigehiro Ozawa, 1974, Japan)
Get Carter (Mike Hodges, 1971, UK)
Godfather, The (Francis Ford Coppola, 1972, US)
Godfather Part II, The (Francis Ford Coppola, 1974, US)
GoodFellas (Martin Scorsese, 1990, US)
Great Train Robbery, The (Edwin S. Porter, 1903, US)
Grindhouse (Robert Rodriguez and Quentin Tarantino, 2007, US)
Gun Crazy (Joseph H. Lewis, 1950, US)
Halloween (John Carpenter, 1978, US)
Häxan/The Witch (Benjamin Christensen, 1922, Denmark/Sweden)
Hei tai yang 731/Men Behind the Sun (Tun Fei Mou, 1988, Hong Kong)
Henry: Portrait of a Serial Killer (John McNaughton, 1986, US)
Horrors of the Black Museum (Arthur Crabtree, 1959, UK)
Hostel (Eli Roth, 2005, US)
I quattro dell'apocalisse/Four for the Apocalypse (Lucio Fulchi, 1975, Italy)
Idi i smotri/Come and See (Elem Klimov, 1985, Soviet Union)
If... (Lindsay Anderson, 1968, UK)
Il buono, il brutto, il cattivo/The Good, the Bad, and the Ugly (Sergio Leone, 1966, Italy/Spain/West Germany)

In Cold Blood (Richard Brooks, 1967, US)
Indiana Jones and the Temple of Doom (Steven Spielberg, 1984, US)
Intolerance (D. W. Griffith, 1916, US)
Irréversible (Gaspar Noé, 2002, France)
Jaws (Steven Spielberg, 1975, US)
Jigoku (Nobuo Nakagawa, 1960, Japan)
Joe (John G. Avildsen, 1970, US)
Jungfrukällan/The Virgin Spring (Ingmar Bergman, 1960, Sweden)
Kanal (Andrzej Wajda, 1957, Poland)
Kill Bill Vol. 1 (Quentin Tarantino, 2004, US)
Kill Bill Vol. 2 (Quentin Tarantino, 2005, US)
Killers, The (Don Siegel, 1964, US)
Kiss Me Deadly (Robert Aldrich, 1955, US)
Kiss of Death (Henry Hathaway, 1947, US)
Koroshiya 1/Ichi the Killer (Takashi Miike, 2001, Japan/Hong Kong/South
　Korea)
La haine (Mathieu Kassovitz, 1995, France)
Last House on the Left, The (Wes Craven, 1972, US)
Lat sau san taam/Hard-Boiled (John Woo, 1992, Hong Kong)
Le bourreau turc/The Terrible Turkish Executioner (Georges Méliès, 1904,
　France)
Les derniers moments d'Anne de Boleyn (Georges Méliès, 1905, France)
Les yeux sans visage/Eyes Without a Face (Georges Franju, 1960, France)
Little Caesar (Mervyn LeRoy, 1931, US)
Lock, Stock and Two Smoking Barrels (Guy Ritchie, 1998, UK)
Lord of the Rings: The Fellowship of the Ring, The (Peter Jackson, 2001, US/
　New Zealand)
Lord of the Rings: The Return of the King, The (Peter Jackson, 2003, US/
　New Zealand)
Lord of the Rings: The Two Towers, The (Peter Jackson, 2002, US/New Zealand)
Manchurian Candidate, The (John Frankenheimer, 1962, US)
Maniac (William Lustig, 1980, US)
M*A*S*H (Robert Altman, 1970, US)
Matrix, The (Andy and Larry Wachowski, 1999, US/Australia)
Mean Streets (Martin Scorsese, 1973, US)
Menace II Society (Allen and Albert Hughes, 1993, US)
Midnight Express (Alan Parker, 1978, UK/US)
Monty Python and the Holy Grail (Terry Gilliam and Terry Jones, 1975, UK)
Murders in the Rue Morgue (Robert Florey, 1932, US)

Musketeers of Pig Alley, The (D. W. Griffith, 1912, US)

Naked Prey, The (Cornel Wilde, 1966, South Africa/US)

Natural Born Killers (Oliver Stone, 1994, US)

Night of the Living Dead (George A. Romero, 1968, US)

No Country for Old Men (Joel and Ethan Coen, 2007, US)

Oldboy (Chan-wook Park, 2003, South Korea)

One-Eyed Jacks (Marlon Brando, 1961, US)

Passion of the Christ, The (Mel Gibson, 2004, US)

Peeping Tom (Michael Powell, 1959, UK)

Per qualche dollaro in più/For a Few Dollars More (Sergio Leone, 1965, Italy/Spain/West Germany)

Per un pugno di dollari/A Fistful of Dollars (Sergio Leone, 1964, Italy/Spain/West German)

Platoon (Oliver Stone, 1986, US)

Point Blank (John Boorman, 1967, US)

Pride of the Marines (Delmer Daves, 1945, US)

Psycho (Alfred Hitchcock, 1960, US)

Public Enemy, The (William A. Wellman, 1931, US)

Pulp Fiction (Quentin Tarantino, 1994, US)

Raging Bull (Martin Scorsese, 1980, US)

Rambo (Sylvester Stallone, 2008, US/Germany)

Rambo: First Blood Part II (George P. Cosmatos, 1985, US)

Re-Animator (Stuart Gordon, 1985, US)

Rear Window (Alfred Hitchcock, 1954, US)

Red Dawn (John Milius, 1984, US)

Repulsion (Roman Polanski, 1965, UK)

Reservoir Dogs (Quentin Tarantino, 1992, US)

RoboCop (Paul Verhoeven, 1987, US)

Rosewood (John Singleton, 1996, US)

Salò o le 120 giornate di Sodoma/Saló, the 120 Days of Sodom (Pier Paolo Pasolini, 1975, Italy/France)

Saving Private Ryan (Steven Spielberg, 1998, US)

Saw (James Wan, 2004, US/Australia)

Scarface (Howard Hawks, 1932, US)

Scarface (Brian De Palma, 1983, US)

Schindler's List (Steven Spielberg, 1993, US)

Scum of the Earth (Herschell Gordon Lewis, 1963, US)

Searchers, The (John Ford, 1956, US)

Sei donne per l'assassino/Blood and Black Lace (Mario Bava, 1964, Italy/
France/West Germany)

Seven (David Fincher, 1995, US)

Shaft (Gordon Parks, 1971, US)

Shane (George Stevens, 1953, US)

Shichinin no samurai/Seven Samurai (Akira Kurosawa, 1954, Japan)

Shooting Captured Insurgents (Edison Company, 1898, US)

Show Them No Mercy! (George Marshall, 1935, US)

Silence of the Lambs, The (Jonathan Demme, 1991, US)

Sisters (Brian De Palma, 1973, US)

Snuff (Michael Findlay and Roberta Findlay and Horacio Fredriksson,
1976, Argentina/US)

Soldier Blue (Ralph Nelson, 1970, US)

Spartacus (Stanley Kubrick, 1960, US)

Starship Troopers (Paul Verhoeven, 1997, US)

Straw Dogs (Sam Peckinpah, 1971, UK)

Suspiria (Dario Argento, 1977, Italy)

Sweet Sweetback's Baadasssss Song (Mario Van Peebles, 1971, US)

Targets (Peter Bogdanovich, 1968, US)

Taxi Driver (Martin Scorsese, 1976, US)

Terminator 2: Judgment Day (James Cameron, 1991, US)

Texas Chainsaw Massacre, The (Marcus Nispel, 2003, US)

Texas Chain Saw Massacre, The (Tobe Hooper, 1974, US)

Three Kings (David O. Russell, 1999, US)

Tôkyô zankoku keisatsu/Tokyo Gore Police (Yoshihiro Nishimura, 2008,
Japan)

True Romance (Tony Scott, 1993, US)

Tsubaki Sanjûrô/Sanjuro (Akira Kurosawa, 1962, Japan)

Two Thousand Maniacs (Herschell Gordon Lewis, 1964, US)

Un chien andalou (Luis Buñuel, 1929, France)

Unforgiven (Clint Eastwood, 1992, US)

Wild Bunch, The (Sam Peckinpah, 1969, US)

Witchfinder General (Michael Reeves, 1968, UK)

Within Our Gates (Oscar Micheaux, 1919, US)

Yojimbo (Akira Kurosawa, 1961, Japan)

BIBLIOGRAPHY

Abel, Richard (1994) *The Ciné Goes to Town: French Cinema 1896–1914*. Berkeley: University of California Press.

Alloway, Lawrence (1971) *Violent America: The Movies 1946–1964*. New York: Museum of Modern Art.

Altman, Rick (1995 [1984]) 'A Semantic/Syntactic Approach to Film Genre', in Barry Keith Grant (ed.) *Film Genre Reader II*. Austin: University of Texas Press, 26–40.

____ (1999) *Film Genre*. London: British Film Institute.

Anderson, Christopher (1994) *Hollywood TV: The Studio System in the Fifties*. Austin: University of Texas Press.

Anon. (1915) 'Growth of the Movies', *New York Times*, 31 October, 16.

____ (1923) 'Witchcraft', *Variety*, 30 August, 30.

____ (1948) 'Comic Book Action Set: Parent-Teacher Group to Fight "Vicious" Entertainment Media', *New York Times,* 12 November, 29.

____ (1960) 'Cinema: The New Pictures', *Time,* 24 October.

On-line. Available at: http://www.time.com/time/magazine/article/0,9171,871800,00.html (accessed 10 August 2009).

____ (1969) 'Press Violent About Film's Violence, Prod Sam Peckinpah Following "Bunch"', *Variety*, 2 July, 15.

Armstrong, Nancy and Leonard Tennenhouse (1989) 'Introduction: Representing Violence, or "How the West Was Won"', in Nancy Armstrong and Leonard Tennenhouse (eds) *The Violence of Representation: Literature and the History of Violence*. London: Routledge, 1–28.

Arroyo, José (ed.) (2000) *Action/Spectacle Cinema: A Sight and Sound Reader*. London: British Film Institute.

Atkins, Thomas R. (ed.) (1976) *Graphic Violence on the Screen*. New York: Monarch Press.

Bailey, John (1994) 'Bang Bang Bang Band, Ad Nauseum', *American Cinematographer,* 75, 12, 26–9.

Barker, Martin (1995) 'Violence', *Sight & Sound,* 5, 6, 10–13.

____ (1997) 'The Newsom Report: A Case Study in "Common Sense"', in Martin Barker and Judith Petley (eds) *Ill Effects: The Media/Violence Debate*. London: Routledge, 12–31.

____ (2004) 'Violence redux', in Steven Jay Schneider (ed.) *New Hollywood Violence*. Manchester: Manchester University Press, 57–79.

Bennett, Tony and Janet Woollacott (1987) *Beyond Bond: The Political Career of a Popular Hero*. London: Macmillan Education.

Berenstein, Rhona J. (1996) *Attack of the Leading Ladies: Gender, Sexuality, and Spectatorship in Classic Horror Cinema*. New York: Columbia University Press.

Berg, Chuck (2000) 'Fade-Out in the West: The Western's Last Stand?', in Wheeler Winston Dixon (ed.) *Film Genre 2000*. Albany: State University of New York Press, 211–25.

Biskind, Peter (2004) *Down and Dirty Pictures: Miramax, Sundance, and the Rise of Independent Film*. New York: Simon & Schuster.

Black, Gregory D. (1997) *The Catholic Crusade Against the Movies, 1940–1975*. New York: Cambridge University Press.

Black, Joel (2002a) *The Reality Effect: Film Culture and the Graphic Imperative*. New York: Routledge.

____ (2002b) 'Real(ist) Horror: From Execution Videos to Snuff Films', in Xavier Mendik and Steven Jay Schneider (eds) *Underground U.S.A.: Filmmaking Beyond the Hollywood Cannon*. London: Wallflower Press, 63–75.

Bok, Sissela (1998) *Mayhem: Violence as Public Entertainment*. Reading, MA: Addison-Wesley.

Bouzereau, Laurent (1996) *Ultraviolent Movies: From Sam Peckinpah to Quentin Tarantino*. Secaucus, NJ: Citadel Press.

Brandon, Craig (1999) *The Electric Chair: An Unnatural American History*. Jefferson, NC: McFarland.

Brite, Poppy Z. (1996) 'The Poetry of Violence', in Karl French (ed.) *Screen Violence*. New York: Bloomsbury, 62–70.

Brottman, Mikita (1995) 'Carnivalizing the Taboo: The Mondo Film and the Opened Body', *Cineaction*, 38, 25–37.

____ (2005) *Offensive Films*. Nashville, TN: Vanderbilt University Press.

Brownlow, Kevin (1990) *Behind the Mask of Innocence*. New York: Knopf.

Buckley, Peter (1971) 'Review: *Soldier Blue*', *Films and Filming*, 17, 9, 65–6.

Butler, Ivan (1971) *Horror in the Cinema*. New York: Paperback Library.

Butters, Jr, Gerald R. (2000) 'From Homestead to Lynch Mob: Portrayals of Black Masculinity in Oscar Micheaux's *Within Our Gates*', *Journal for Multimedia History*, 3. On-line. Available at: http://www.albany.edu/jmmh/vol3/micheaux/micheaux.html (accessed 10 August 2009).

Bygrave, Mike (2003) 'Quentin
Tarantino: Freak Thrills',
Independent, 20 July, 21.

Cawelti, John G. (1971) *The Six-Gun
Mystique*. Bowling Green, OH:
Bowling Green University Popular
Press.

____ (1984) *The Six-Gun Mystique*,
second edition. Bowling Green,
OH: Bowling Green University
Popular Press.

Chapman, James (2000) *License to
Thrill: A Cultural History of the
James Bond Films*. New York:
Columbia University Press.

Christie, Ian (1978) 'The Scandal of
Peeping Tom', in Ian Christie (ed.)
Powell, Pressburger, and Others.
London: British Film Institute,
53–9.

Cisin, Ira H., Thomas E. Coffin, Irvin L.
Janis, Joseph T. Klapper, Harold
Mendelsohn, Eveline Omwake,
Charles A. Pinderhughes, Ithiel
de Sola Pool, Alberta E. Siegel,
Anthony F. C. Wallace, Andrew
S. Watson and Gerhart D. Wiebe
(1972) *Television and Growing Up:
The Impact of Televised Violence.
Report to the Surgeon General
United States Public Health
Service*. Washington, DC: US
Government Printing Office.

Clarens, Carlos (1967) *An Illustrated
History of Horror and Science-
Fiction Films: The Classic Era,
1895–1967*. New York: De Capo
Press.

Clover, Carol (1992) *Men, Women,
and Chain Saws: Gender in the
Modern Horror Film*. Princeton, NJ:
Princeton University Press.

Cook, David A. (1983) '*The Wild Bunch*,
Fifteen Years After', *North Dakota
Quarterly*, 51, 123–30.

____ (1998) 'Auteur Cinema and
the "Film Generation" in 1970s
Hollywood', in Jon Lewis (ed.) *The
New American Cinema*. Durham,
NC: Duke University Press, 11–37.

____ (1999) 'Ballistic Balletics: Styles
of Violent Representations in *The
Wild Bunch* and After', in Stephen
Prince (ed.) *Sam Peckinpah's The
Wild Bunch*. Cambridge: Cambridge
University Press, 130–54.

____ (2000) *Lost Illusions: American
Cinema in the Shadow of
Watergate and Vietnam,
1970–1979* (History of the
American Cinema, Vol. 9).
Berkeley: University of California
Press.

Crowdus, Gary and Richard Porton
(1994) 'The Importance of a
Singular, Guiding Vision: An
Interview with Arthur Penn',
Cineaste, 20, 2, 4–16.

Crowther, Bosley (1955) 'Screen:
Disney and the Coonskin Set;
"Davy Crockett" Fights Again at the
Globe; Fess Parker Plays King of
the Wild Frontier', *New York Times*,
26 May, 36.

____ (1967a) 'Another Smash at
Violence', *New York Times*, 30
July, 69.

____ (1967b) 'Screen: *Bonnie and
Clyde* Arrives', *New York Times*, 14
August, 36.

Curry, Christopher Wayne (2000) *A Taste of Blood: The Films of Herschell Gordon Lewis*. London: Creation Books.

Doherty, Thomas (1988) *Teenagers and Teenpics: The Juvenilization of American Movies in the 1950s*. Boston: Unwin Hyman.

____ (1999) *Pre-Code Hollywood: Sex, Immorality, and Insurrection in American Cinema 1930–1934*. New York: Columbia University Press.

Ebert, Roger (1974) 'Review of *The Texas Chain Saw Massacre*', *Chicago Sun-Times*. On-line. Available at: http://rogerebert. suntimes.com/apps/pbcs. dll/article?AID=/19740101/ REVIEWS/401010319/1023 (accessed 3 October 2009).

Eisenstein, Sergei (1957 [1949]) 'A Dialectic Approach to Film Form', in *Film Form: Essays in Film Theory*, trans. Jay Leyda. New York: Meridian Books, 45–63.

Eisner, Lotte H. (1973) *The Haunted Screen: Expressionism in the German Cinema and the Influence of Max Reinhardt*. Berkeley: University of California Press.

Farber, Stephen (1969) 'Peckinpah's Return', *Film Quarterly*, 23, 2–11.

____ (1972) *The Movie Rating Game*. Washington, DC: Public Affairs Press.

Feshbach, Seymour (1955) 'The Drive-Reducing Function of Fantasy Behavior', *Journal of Abnormal and Social Psychology*, 50, 1, 3–11.

Forman, Henry James (1933) *Our Movie Made Children*. New York: Macmillan.

Fraser, John (1974) *Violence in the Arts*, illustrated edition. London: Cambridge University Press.

French, Karl (ed.) (1996) *Screen Violence*. London: Bloomsbury.

French, Philip (1968) 'Violence in the Cinema', in O. N. Larsen (ed.) *Violence and the Mass Media*. New York: Harper & Row, 59–70.

Gerbner, George and Larry Gross (1976) 'Living With Television: The Violence Profile', *Journal of Communication*, 26, 2, 172–99.

Gerbner, George, Larry Gross, Michael Morgan and Nancy Signorielli (1994) 'Growing Up With Television: The Cultivation Perspective', in Jennings Bryant and Dolf Zillman (eds) *Media Effects: Advances in Theorye and Research*. Hillsdale, NJ: Erlbaum, 17–43.

Giroux, Henry A. (1996) *Fugitive Cultures: Race, Violence, and Youth*. New York: Routledge.

Goldstein, Jeffrey H. (ed.) (1998) *Why We Watch: The Attractions of Violent Entertainment*. New York: Oxford University Press.

Grant, Barry Keith (1995) 'Introduction', in Barry Keith Grant (ed.) *Film Genre Reader II*. Austin: University of Texas Press, xv–xx.

Gross, Larry (2000) 'Big and Loud', in José Arroyo (ed.) *Action/Spectacle Cinema: A Sight and Sound Reader*. London: British Film Institute, 3–8.

Guerrero, Ed (2001) 'Black Violence as Cinema: From Cheap Thrills to Historical Agonies', in J. David Slocum (ed.) *Violence and American Cinema*. New York: Routledge, 211–25.

Harmetz, Aljean (1969) '"Man Was a Killer Long Before He Served a God"', *New York Times*, 31 August, D9.

Hawkins, Joan (2000) *Cutting Edge: Art-Horror and the Horrific Avant-Garde*. Minneapolis: University of Minnesota Press.

Higgins, Scott and Sara Ross (2007) 'Archival News', *Cinema Journal*, 46, 4, 133–44.

Hill, Annette (1997) *Shocking Entertainment: Viewer Response to Violent Movies*. Bedfordshire: University of Luton Press.

Hoberman, J. (1998) '"A Test for the Individual Viewer": *Bonnie and Clyde*'s Violence Reception', in Jeffrey H. Goldstein (ed.) *Why We Watch: The Attractions of Violent Entertainment*. New York: Oxford University Press, 116–43.

Hoberman, J. and Jonathan Rosenbaum (1983) *Midnight Movies*. New York: Harper & Row.

Horsley, Jake (1999a) *The Blood Poets: A Cinema of Savagery 1958–1999. Vol. I: American Chaos – From Touch of Evil to The Terminator*. Lanham, MD: Scarecrow Press.

_____ (1999b) *The Blood Poets: A Cinema of Savagery 1958–1999. Vol. II: Millennial Blues – From Apocalypse Now to The Matrix*, Lanham, MD: Scarecrow Press.

Houseman, John (1947) 'Violence, 1947: Three Specimens', *Hollywood Quarterly*, 3, 1, 63–5.

Hunter, Stephen (1995) *Violent Screen*. New York: Delta.

Jeffords, Susan (1989) *The Remasculinization of America: Gender and the Vietnam War*. Bloomington: Indiana University Press.

_____ (1994) *Hard Bodies: Hollywood Masculinity in the Reagan Era*. New Brunswick, NJ: Rutgers University Press.

Jenkins, Henry (2002) 'Coming Up Next: Ambushed on "Donahue"!' *Salon*, 20 August. On-line. Available at: http://dir.salon.com/story/tech/feature/2002/08/20/jenkins_on_donahue/index.html (accessed 17 August 2009).

Jonas, Gerald (1975) 'The Man Who Gave an "X" Rating to Violence', *New York Times*, 11 May, D1.

Jones, Jenny M. (2007) *The Annotated Godfather: The Complete Screenplay With Commentary on Every Scene, Interviews, and Little-Known Facts*. New York: Black Dog & Leventhal.

Jowett, Garth S. (1971) 'Books', *Film Comment*, 7, 1, 70–2.

Kael, Pauline (1968) *Kiss Kiss Bang Bang*. New York: Bantham.

_____ (1994) *For Keeps: 30 Years at the Movies*. New York: Plume.

Kaminsky, Stuart M. (1976) 'Italian Westerns and Kung Fu Films: Genres of Violence', in Thomas R. Atkins (ed.) *Graphic Violence on the Screen*. New York: Monarch Press, 47–68.

Kauffman, Stanley (1960) 'Several Sons, Several Lovers', *New Republic,* 29 August, 21–2.

Kendrick, James (2004) 'A Nasty Situation: Social Panics, Transnationalism, and the Video Nasty', in Steffen Hantke (ed.) *Horror Film: Creating and Marketing Fear.* Jackson: University Press of Mississippi, 153–72.

____ (2009) *Hollywood Bloodshed: Violence in 1980s American Cinema.* Carbondale: Southern Illinois University Press.

Kendrick, Walter (1991) *The Thrill of Fear: 250 Years of Scary Entertainment.* New York: Grove Weidenfeld.

Kerkes, David and David Slater (1994) *Killing for Culture: An Illustrated History of Death Film From Mondo to Snuff.* London: Creation Books.

Kermode, Mark (1997a) '"I Was a Teenage Horror Fan": or, "How I Learned to Stop Worrying and Love Linda Blair"', in Martin Barker and Julian Petley (eds) *Ill Effects: The Media/Violence Debate.* London: Routledge, 57–66.

____ (1997b) 'Horror: On the Edge of Taste', in Ruth Petrie (ed.) *Film and Censorship.* London: Cassell, 155–60.

King, Geoff (2004) '"Killingly Funny": Mixing Modalities in New Hollywood's Comedy-With-Violence', in Steven Jay Schneider (ed.) *New Hollywood Violence.* Manchester: Manchester University Press, 126–43.

Kolker, Robert (2000) *A Cinema of Loneliness: Penn, Stone, Kubrick, Scorsese, Spielberg, Altman,* third edition. New York: Oxford University Press.

Lange, David L., Robert K. Baker and Sandra J. Ball (1969) *Mass Media and Violence: A Report to the National Commission on the Causes and Prevention of Violence* (Vol. XI). Washington, DC: US Government Printing Office.

Leach, Michael (1975) *I Know It When I See It: Pornography, Violence, and Public Sensitivity.* Philadelphia: Westminster Press.

Leff, Leonard J. and Jerold L. Simmons (1990) *The Dame in the Kimono: Hollywood, Censorship, and the Production Code from the 1920s to the 1960s.* New York: Anchor Books.

Leitch, Thomas (2004) 'Aristotle v. the Action Film', in Steven Jay Schneider (ed.) *New Hollywood Violence.* Manchester: Manchester University Press, 103–25.

Lev, Peter (2000) *American Films of the 70s: Conflicting Visions.* Austin: University of Texas Press.

Lewis, Jon (2000) *Hollywood v. Hard Core: How the Struggle Over Censorship Saved the Modern Film Industry.* New York: New York University Press.

Lichtenfeld, Eric (2004) *Action Speaks Louder: Violence, Spectacle, and the American Action Movie.* Westport, CT: Praeger.

____ (2007) 'Yippee-Ki-Yay...: The Greatest One-Liner in Movie

History', *Slate,* 26 June. On-line. Available at: http://www.slate.com/id/2168927 (accessed 17 August 2009).

Lu, Weiting, David Waterman and Michael Zhaoxu Yan (2006) 'An Economic Study of Violence in Motion Pictures: Genre Trends and Technological Change', in *Conference Papers: International Communication Association, 2006 Annual Meeting,* 1–24.

Lyons, Charles (1997) *The New Censors: Movies and the Culture Wars.* Philadelphia, PA: Temple University Press.

Maltby, Richard (1995) 'Documents of the Production Code', *Quarterly Review of Film & Video,* 15, 4, 33–63.

_____ (2001) 'The Spectacle of Criminality', in J. David Slocum (ed.) *Violence and American Cinema.* New York: Routledge, 117–52.

Martin, Olga J. (1937) *Hollywood's Movie Commandments: A Handbook for Motion Picture Writers and Reviewers.* New York: H. W. Wilson.

Mathews, Tom Dewe (1994) *Censored: The Story of Film Censorship in Britain.* London: Chatto & Windus.

McCarty, John (1984) *Splatter Movies: Breaking the Last Taboo of the Screen.* New York: St. Martin's Press.

McDonagh, Maitland (1994) *Broken Mirrors/Broken Minds: The Dark Dreams of Dario Argento.* New York: Citadel Press.

McGilligan, Patrick (2007) *The Great and Only Oscar Micheaux: The Life of America's First Black Filmmaker.* New York: HarperCollins.

McKinney, Devin (1993) 'Violence: The Strong and the Weak', *Film Quarterly,* 46, 4, 16–22.

Merrill, Robert and John L. Simons (1994) 'The Waking Nightmare of Mike Nichols' *Catch-22*', in Barbara Tepa Lupack (ed.) *Take Two: Adapting the Contemporary American Novel to Film.* Bowling Green, OH: Bowling Green State University Popular Press, 16–35.

Metz, Christian (1974) *Film Language: A Semiotics of the Cinema,* trans. Michael Taylor. New York: Oxford University Press.

Miller, Frank (1994) *Censored Hollywood: Sex, Sin, & Violence on Screen.* Atlanta, GA: Turner.

Mirams, Gordon (1951) 'Drop That Gun!', *Quarterly Review of Film, Radio, and Television,* 6, 1, 1–19.

Mitchell, Lee Clark (2001) 'Violence in the Film Western', in J. David Slocum (ed.) *Violence and American Cinema.* New York: Routledge, 176–91.

Morgenstern, Joe (1968) 'The Thin Red Line', *Newsweek,* 28 August, 82–3.

Muller, Eddie and Daniel Faris (1996) *Grindhouse: The Forbidden World of 'Adults Only' Cinema.* New York: St. Martin's Press.

Munby, Jonathan (1999) *Public Enemies, Public Heroes: Screening the Gangster From Little Caesar to Touch of Evil.* Chicago: University of Chicago Press.

Musser, Charles (1990) *The Emergence of Cinema: The American Screen to 1907*. Berkeley: University of California Press.

Naremore, James (1998) *More Than Night: Film Noir in Its Contexts*. Berkeley: University of California Press.

Neale, Steve (1983) 'Masculinity as Spectacle: Reflections on Men and Mainstream Cinema', *Screen*, 24, 6, 2–17.

____ (1995 [1990]) 'Questions of Genre', in Barry Keith Grant (ed.) *Film Genre Reader II*. Austin: University of Texas Press, 159–83.

____ (2000) *Genre and Hollywood*. London: Routledge.

Nelson, Ralph (1970) 'Massacre at Sand Creek', *Films and Filming*, 16, 6, 26–7.

Oberbeck, S. K. (1970) 'US Cavalry Go Home', *Newsweek*, 24 August, 65.

Panofksy, Erwin (1951) 'Style and Medium in the Motion Pictures', in Eric Bentley (ed.) *The Play: A Critical Anthology*. New York: Prentice-Hall, 751–72.

Parker, Alison M. (1996) 'Mothering the Movies: Women Reformers and Popular Culture', in Francis G. Couvares (ed.) *Movie Censorship and American Culture*. Washington, DC: Smithsonian Institution Press, 73–96.

Paul, William (1994) *Laughing, Screaming: Modern Hollywood Horror & Comedy*. New York: Columbia University Press.

Philips, Baxter (1975) *Cut: The Unseen Cinema*. New York: Bounty Books.

Plagens, Peter, Mark Miller, Donna Foote and Emily Yoffe (1991) 'Violence in Our Culture', *Newsweek*, 1 April, 46–52.

Plantinga, Carl (1998) 'Spectacles of Death: Clint Eastwood and Violence in *Unforgiven*', *Cinema Journal*, 37, 2, 65–83.

Pomerance, Murray (2004) 'Hitchcock and the Dramaturgy of Screen Violence', in Stephen Jay Schneider (ed.) *New Hollywood Violence*. Manchester: Manchester University Press, 34–56.

Prince, Stephen (1998) *Savage Cinema: Sam Peckinpah and the Rise of Ultraviolent Movies*. New Brunswick, NJ: Rutgers University Press.

____ (2000a) 'Graphic Violence in the Cinema: Origins, Aesthetic Design, and Social Effects', in Stephen Prince (ed.) *Screening Violence*. New Brunswick, NJ: Rutgers University Press, 1–46.

____ (ed.) (2000b) *Screening Violence*. New Brunswick, NJ: Rutgers University Press.

____ (2003) *Classical Film Violence: Designing and Regulating Brutality in Hollywood Cinema, 1930–1968*. New Brunswick, NJ: Rutgers University Press.

____ (2006) 'Beholding Blood Sacrifice in *The Passion of the Christ*: How Real is Movie Violence?', *Film Quarterly*, 59, 4, 11–22.

Pritchard, Harriet S. (1914) 'A Federal Motion Picture Commission', *Signal*, 21 May, 10.

Rader, Dotson (1970) 'Who Were the Bad Guys?', *New York Times*, 20 September, Section II, 13.

Rich, B. Ruby (1992) 'Art House Killers', *Sight and Sound*, 2, 8, 5–6.

Ronan, Margaret (1970) 'Blood Red', *Senior Scholastic*, 5 October, 20–1.

Sandler, Kevin S. (2007) *The Naked Truth: Why Hollywood Doesn't Make X-Rated Movies*. New Brunswick, NJ: Rutgers University Press.

Schaefer, Eric (1999) *Bold! Daring! Shocking! True! A History of Exploitation Films, 1919–1959*. Durham, NC: Duke University Press.

Schatz, Thomas (1981) *Hollywood Genres: Formulas, Filmmaking, and the Studio System*. Austin: University of Texas Press.

____ (1992) 'The New Hollywood', in Jim Collins, Hilary Radner and Ava Preaders Collins (eds) *Film Theory Goes to the Moves*. New York: Routledge, 8–36.

Schechter, Harold (2005) *Savage Pastimes: A Cultural History of Violent Entertainment*. New York: St. Martin's Press.

Schneider, Steven Jay (ed.) (2004) *New Hollywood Violence*. Manchester: Manchester University Press.

Schubart, Rikke (2001) 'Passion and Acceleration: Generic Change in the Action Film', in J. David Slocum (ed.) *Violence and American Cinema*. New York: Routledge, 192–207.

Shachtman, Tom (1983) *Decade of Shocks: Dallas to Watergate, 1963–1974*. New York: Poseidon Press.

Slocum, J. David (2001) 'Introduction: Violence and American Cinema: Notes for an Investigation', in J. David Slocum (ed.) *Violence and American Cinema*. New York: Routledge, 1–36.

Slotkin, Richard (1973) *Regeneration Through Violence: The Mythology of the American Frontier, 1600–1860*. Middletown, CT: Wesleyan University Press.

Smith, Margaret Chase (1967) '"Sick Movies" – A Menace to Children', *Reader's Digest*, December, 139–42.

Sobchack, Thomas (1995 [1975]) 'Genre Film: A Classical Experience', in Barry Keith Grant (ed.) *Film Genre Reader II*. Austin: University of Texas Press, 102–13.

Sobchack, Vivian C. (1976) 'The Violent Dance: A Personal Memoir of Death in the Movies', in Thomas R. Atkins (ed.) *Graphic Violence on the Screen*. New York: Monarch Press, 79–94.

____ (2000) 'Afterword: The Postmorbid Condition', in Stephen Prince (ed.) *Screening Violence*. New Brunswick, NJ: Rutgers University Press, 119–24.

Spehr, Paul C. (2001) 'Unaltered to Date: Developing 35mm Film', in John Fullerton and Astrid Soderbergh-Widding (eds) *Moving Image: From Edison to the Webcam*. Bloomington: Indiana University Press, 3–28.

Streible, Dan (1989) 'A History of the Boxing Film, 1894–1915: Social Control and Social Reform in the Progressive Era', *Film History,* 3, 3, 235–57.

Taylor, John (1989) *Circus of Ambition: The Culture of Wealth and Power in the Eighties*. New York: Warner Books.

Waller, Gregory A. (2000 [1987]) 'Introduction to *American Horrors*', in Ken Gelder (ed.) *The Horror Reader*. New York: Routledge, 256–64.

Walsh, Moira (1970) 'More Loathsome Films', *America,* 19 September, 185–6.

Waterman, David (2005) *Hollywood's Road to Riches*. Cambridge: Harvard University Press.

Wertham, Frederic (1954) *Seduction of the Innocent*. New York: Rinehart.

Williams, Christopher (ed.) (1980) *Realism and the Cinema: A Reader*. London: Routledge.

Williams, Linda (1994) 'Learning to Scream', *Sight and Sound,* 4, 12, 14–17.

____ (1995 [1991]) 'Film Bodies: Gender, Genre, Excess', in Barry Keith Grant (ed.) *Film Genre Reader II*. Austin: University of Texas Press, 140–58.

Witcombe, Rick Trader (1975) *Savage Cinema*. London: Lorrimer.

Wood, Robin (1996 [1979]) 'An Introduction to the American Horror Film', in Barry Keith Grant (ed.) *Planks of Reason: Essays on the Horror Film*. Lanham, MD: Scarecrow Press, 164–200.

Wright, Judith Hess (1995 [1974]) 'Genre Films and the Status Quo', in Barry Keith Grant (ed.) *Film Genre Reader II*. Austin: University of Texas Press, 41–9.

Wright, Will (1975) *Sixguns & Society: A Structural Study of the Western*. Berkeley: University of California Press.

Wyatt, Justin (1994) *High Concept: Movies and Marketing in Hollywood*. Austin: University of Texas Press.

Yacowar, Maurice (1993) *The Films of Paul Morrissey*. New York: Cambridge University Press.

Zillmann, Dolf (1998) 'The Psychology of the Appeals of the Portrayals of Violence', in Jeffrey H. Goldstein (ed.) *Why We Watch: The Attractions of Violent Entertainment*. New York: Oxford University Press, 179–211.

INDEX